MEDITERRANEAN MOTHERS

masters

of

guilt

MEDITERRANEAN MOTHERS

masters
of
guilt

MARIA ORLANDO & NICK PAPPAS

atmosphere press

Published by Atmosphere Press

Cover design by Ronaldo Alves

atmospherepress.com

This book is dedicated to our moms and aunts, who showed us how to use guilt as an art form – but we love you – Maria and Nick

CONTENTS

PROLOGUE

With all due respect to other nationalities and ethnicities who may have claimed to have a monopoly on guilt, their version of it pales before the passion and fear which is a staple in the handbook of an Italian or Greek mother...

"GROWING OLD IS A CURSE;
HAVING KIDS MAKES IT WORSE"

Mediterranean Island Saying....

CHAPTER ONE

Your Kids Never Listen

"Maria, come in here. You gotta see this movie with us. What are you doing in there? Maria, do you hear me?" Shaking her head, she turns to her sister to make a point: "Liz, they never listen. Your children never listen."

Elizabeth somehow nods her head and shakes it at the same time.

"Mare, you are preaching to the choir. Don't I know it! It's the truth, the absolute truth." She crosses herself and keeps shaking her head.

The speakers? Sisters, two Italian(Sicilian) mothers, both around sixtyish, give or take. The place is Marie's house in a quiet town in New Jersey. She and her older sister are about to watch *MARTY*, starring Ernest Borgnine.

The younger of the two, Marie, is Maria's mother. The age difference between her and her sister Elizabeth is almost exactly seven years. They rarely use their full given names when speaking with each other, but rather "Liz" and "Mare." They are both "old school" Italian mothers when it comes to their perspective on their children, but Marie, the younger sister, fancies herself just a bit more "with it" than Liz, who really couldn't care less about the latest trends in fashion, language, or just about anything else.

"Maria, come watch this with us. Why don't you ever listen to me?"

"Ma, I've seen this movie a dozen times."

"It's a great movie. It's about Italians, like us. It's about Italian mothers whose children won't listen to them. They have no respect for their mothers. It's a sin. Look, it's starting. MARIA!"

Maria knows when she is beaten, so rather than buck her mother some more, she decides to come in from the dining room and watch the movie. It is, after all, one of her favorites, and she figures she can put off her work for an hour or so, and hopefully the minutes invested with her mom and aunt will give her some time to herself on the other side.

"OK, mother, just a minute. I just want to organize my papers here before I come in with you. They're just running the credits now anyway."

"Good. Hurry up. And bring us something to snack on, would you? Something sweet, OK? Maria....(louder) OK?? And don't roll your eyes at us!"

"Ma, you can't see me. How would you know if I rolled my eyes." Maria rolls her eyes again, then gathers her stuff together, and organizes it as efficiently and quickly as she can,, all the while cursing profusely under her breath.

Her mother turns to Elizabeth.

"You see, my daughter had to go to college and become an English teacher. She thinks she's so damn smart. I tell her – just pass all the kids. Who cares? Nobody cared about her when she was going to school. Now she spends all her time correcting all those papers, and she got no time for her mother."

"I know, I know, Mare. When they're small, they need you and they obey most of the time. Now when they're grown, they couldn't care less."

Elizabeth is sitting in a rocking chair, and the louder and quicker the conversation, the faster she rocks. This particular chair used to be her grandmother's in Sicily, and it creaks and squeaks like an old barn door that has never been oiled. It seemed to be held together by masking tape, and it's a wonder someone, namely Liz, hadn't broken her neck on it. But it was almost like a member of the family, and it would have been almost sacrilege not to use it....

"Hey, Liz, , Be careful. You gonna fall..."

"Don't worry for me. This gets out all my worries. You talk, I rock. It's like when we were little and we went on the swings. You stayed low and talked, I went way up in the air."

"Yeah, and you fell out at least once every day. And who brought you in the house and bandaged you up? I did Listen, if you fall you patch yourself up on your own. I want to watch MARTY. It's gonna start any second.. Where's Maria? Maria, come on, you're gonna miss the beginning. And don't forget our snack."

The beleaguered Maria was toying with the idea of throwing all her work into her bag, then jumping into her car and making a break for it. She loved her mother, and her aunt, but some days they were harder to take than usual, and the "usual" was quite intolerable in its own right. But, as she told herself many times, they were getting older and she had to cut them some slack – but God almighty, they were getting worse and worse with each passing year...Actually each passing day. Oh well, she figured she would just bite her tongue and play the dutiful daughter and niece for the afternoon. She did like the movie, and hopefully, she could get back to her stuff afterwards. Although she would probably wind up taking them out for dinner, and that would blow the whole day. Trapped again!

It seemed to Maria that she was always running somewhere for something and usually at the behest of someone else. "Maria, do this. Maria do that. Maria, where are those grades. Maria, get us something to eat." When she was with her mom or her aunt, it seemed she was more of a personal valet than a daughter or a niece. Now, she had some autonomy in school, since in her classroom she was more or less in charge. But the red tape and bureaucratic regulations seemed to have increased exponentially over her thirty years of teaching. Trapped in school, controlled at home. How did things wind up this way? She had always wanted to be a writer — more specifically a travel journalist — but life got In the way, and she wound up teaching English, mostly in New Jersey, but there was also that sojourn in California.

Was she ever really there? It seemed like yesterday and at the same time a hundred years ago...For that matter, was she really here? "Here" being her mother's house where she grew up. It's hard to believe her mother was still living in the same house. The mother of all sighs — infused with years of exasperation — escaped despite her valiant attempt to keep it inside.

"Maria, did you say something?" her mom exclaimed from the living room.

Jesus, there was certainly nothing wrong with her hearing.

"No, Ma, just yawning. Be right there."

"You work too damn hard. Just give them all A's. Who's gonna know?"

Maria almost bit through her tongue so she would not reply. Her mother must have said that to her a hundred times. A hundred times in the last few days. She wondered if all mothers got like that, or if it were just "Mediterranean Mothers," like her mom, her aunt, and the women in the movie. She made a mental note to ask Nick about his mother. That would be Nick Pappas, her lunch duty partner, a full-blooded Greek with all the flaws and emotional excesses of that particular ethnic group. Or was it a separate species? Why in the hell did she ever agree to write a book with him? No, not this book, a book chronicling their sixty-five years of teaching. Well, in all fairness, it *was* a good idea, but she really didn't need another obligation she didn't have time for. Lord!

All these things went racing through her mind as she opened up a package of biscotti and a bottle of Pellegrino for the matinee in the next room. What was the name of that song Nick sent her...*Forgotten Dreams?* That summarized her life in two words. How did he know she would like it — which she did? Even though she and Nick had known each other only a short time, he seemed to "get" who she was. What a scary thought. Meanwhile, she was not as quick with the snacks as she should have been...

"Maria, come on! Where are you?"

"Coming, mother."

She almost took a header on a settee that had no business being where it was, but she managed to steady herself and then navigate the rest of the room without an Incident. She put the biscotti and mineral water on the table. Of course, there was a problem.

"Maria, don't put the cold bottle on my good table. What's the matter with you? You know I have that table for fifty years. Put something under it. You didn't bring any jam for the biscotti? Something to make them sweet?"

Maria only half heard her mother. She had already sat down and was busy ungluing herself from the clear, plastic furniture covers that apparently were required of any household whose owners could trace their roots to the northern shores of the Mediterranean Sea. Why the hell had she worn a dress? They were sticky and hot and gross and as she tried to move one way, her skin seemed not only to be transfixed, but to be moving in the opposite direction, not only defying the laws of physics but causing extreme discomfort.

"For God's sake, Ma, when are you going to get rid of these

damn plastic covers?"

"Well, they have been a lifesaver. They have protected all this furniture for thirty years, and they're still in good shape."

"They've protected it because people don't want to sit on it. Ah, OK, it's your house, I'm sorry I yelled. YEOW...." Maria concluded. Her mother and aunt quickly turned their heads with the same scornful looks.

"That was pain, Mom, pain," she explained, as she finally managed to pull her thigh loose. "Pain!"

It was moments like this when she thought of her friends, most of whom would have taken a shot or two before continuing. But that was not an option, so what would would be the best thing to do? Somehow find a way to calm herself down or smash everything and go home? When she got passionate or angry, Maria's eyes took on a life of their own, and at the moment they were on fire. All this took place in a millisecond, and while pondering her next move her glance fell on a bottle of red wine on the breakfront in the corner of the room. It made her think of Nick, and his incredulity when he found out she didn't drink.

"How the hell can you be a Sicilian and not like – at the very least – red wine?"

"Didn't you tell me that your former writing partner didn't like red wine? And he was Italian, right?"

That shut him up for the moment, but Nick had a nonstop mouth and could be very irritating from time to time – more often than not, actually – but thinking of this little exchange between the two of them calmed her down, and a hint of a smile began to emerge. She considered emailing him later and thanking him, but then she thought better of it. It would just get his damn Greek ego up and running again just as she was beginning the monumental task of toning it down.

So, without missing a beat, Maria turned both her mood and countenance around one hundred eighty degrees.

"Sorry, ma. I'm just edgy from work," she said with a grin. "You put whatever torturous covering you want on your furniture. I'll get some jam for you."

"I told you that you work too hard. It's OK. But don't go yet..first watch this part where the mother gets upset with her children. You can learn something from this.. Go back during the commercial."

"OK, Ma."

Another colleague came to mind. He was also a history teacher and his favorite expression was, "No good deed goes unpunished." Jesus, was he ever right!

CHAPTER TWO

Italians On and Off The Screen

MARTY was Ernest Borgnine's Oscar-winning role, and if you were Italian, or a mother, or both, it was like *your* signature role. It told the story of an Italian, unmarried butcher in the Bronx of the 1950s. He was a pleasant, hard-working guy who was harried by all the older Italian women in the neighborhood because all his siblings were married, which begged the question, "When you gonna get married, Marty?" something he heard many times on any given day. Of course, the person who repeated it the most was his own mother, who also always mentioned the ethnicity of the girl he should find: "Why don't you find nice Italian girl, Marty? There are plenty of nice Italian girls."

Getting Marty married off was only one part of the equation his mother had to solve. She was a widow in her sixties, and worried not only about her son, but about her own future. She had a sister, Catherine, who did not get along with her daughter-in-law, who, along with her husband and young baby, lived with Catherine. Talk about a recipe for disaster! Well, Marie and Elizabeth were also widows in their sixties, and while they didn't have to worry about marrying off their kids or anyone living with them, they could very easily have portrayed these roles on the screen because they saw themselves as playing them out in their own heads and their own lives. This was especially true with regard to listening to your mother, which seemed to be a universal problem among those who traced their heritage to somewhere along the Mediterranean. This movie had been a universal hit and deserved all the accolades it and its star received, and while you didn't have to be Italian (or Greek) to love it, it did seem to resonate more with these two groups, which is fortunate because that is essentially the backstory of this book.

Maria finally got things settled to the satisfaction of the finicky ladies. Two kinds of biscotti and jam had been brought out, and there was a coaster for the bottle of Pellegrino, and there was some dark Turkish coffee, complete with a folded-over tablecloth for protection. Plenty to go around – food, drink, and guilt. On the TV the two sisters were talking about their situation in life, and the buzzwords were "curse" and "old," neatly tucked into the phrase "It's a curse to be old," which was repeated several times in the movie, and then reprised at least a dozen times in the living room.

"You see, Maria! Those two women are right. It is a curse to get old, it's a curse. No one cares about you, everyone thinks you're good for nothing, and your kids grow up and leave you. And you know what's the worst thing? They don't listen to you. You give birth to them and feed them and raise them, and then they spit on you. You sacrifice the best years of your life, and they don't call, and they don't care. I could be dead and buried and no one would ever know. Right, Liz?"

Elizabeth had been rocking faster and faster, and when her sister posed the question she appeared to be approaching the speed of sound, which would have made her the first Italian woman to reach that velocity in recorded history. She put her legs straight down and came to a screeching halt.

"You're damn right, Marie. You wake up one day and you see an old woman in the mirror, just like that Catherine says in the movie. And it's a curse to be a widow. See, she's gonna say it right now – listen." Sure enough, Marty's Aunt Catherine said her lines right on cue: "These are the worst years. I see an old lady in the mirror. It's a curse to be a widow."

Maria couldn't hold her laugh in. Her aunt and her mom knew the lines from the movie the way some people know the lines from *The Honeymooners* – actually, the way she and Nick did. What was also both ironic and "laugh-worthy" was the "sainthood" Italian widows often bestowed on their late husbands, who were considered to be good-for-nothing, arrogant, bossy, and abusive bums when they were alive. Well, everybody's personal stock does seem to go up when they're no longer around. But her frivolity drew cold stares from the two women, and it took quite a bit of explaining to extricate herself from their wrath. Of course, she'd been dealing with this her whole life, but to use a sports analogy, ballplayers slow down as they age, these ladies were getting quicker and more combative as the years progressed. Maria couldn't imagine what they might be like in the future, but right now her problem was calming them down and smoothing out the cornucopia of guilt they were unfolding.

Elizabeth just shook her head and whispered to her sister an upcoming line from Catherine to her sister in the movie about "college girls – one step from the street." Maria pretended not to hear it. What else could she do? She didn't want to start a big hubbub, and to tell the truth she was glad her mother made her watch the movie. It was a nice break from school and from editing what Nick had written for their book. *MARTY* ends happily, as he finds a girl he loves and decides to pursue her, even though his mother doesn't approve because she's not Italian. Nobody's perfect, right?

"Maria, you wanna stay and eat with us? Your husband is

on a business trip, right? So you stay and eat with us."

Translation: "let's go out to eat."

Marie had quit cooking quite a while ago, a decision commemorated by a gift from her daughter – a plaque: KITCHEN CLOSED – THIS CHICK HAS HAD IT!

Now, Maria had no problem having dinner with her mom and aunt, as long as they let her pick the place. That way she could be sure the food was OK and the ladies would like the accouterments. She figured they may as well go to a diner. As far as getting any work done, the day was pretty well shot, and it was good to get them out of the house, especially this house, the same house where Maria grew up and where her mother had lived for the better part of five decades.

CHAPTER THREE

"Nobody Bothers Me Here"

Ah, the house. Maria and her two siblings had grown up here. There were holidays, and birthdays, happy, carefree days, and sad days, like when her father died. There seemed to be a memory in every room, and, while life does go on and change is indeed a necessary part of it, just as the ladies in the movie, her mother was used to living there and took offense at any suggestion to the contrary. Guilt trips notwithstanding, Maria was a fairly regular visitor, and there was always something that had to be addressed or looked into or argued over. Always. It was a stately, impressive looking home, built in a neighborhood of similarly traditional but unique structures, in what had been an area that, while not exclusive, showed that the families who lived here had done pretty well for themselves.

The inside was welcoming and familiar, a place that had served the family well for almost fifty years. The decor was more or less Italian, with its mixture of art and stone, paintings, sofas and tables of all sorts, and scores and scores of family pictures. Even with the "super glue" plastic on the upholstered chairs, everything seemed to echo the words "come and sit and visit." Her mother always kept it up nicely, but now that she was getting older, neatness was no longer a priority and there were piles of things in various places, and chairs set up where no one would ever sit. The neighborhood was also different, as people raised their families and moved, so her mother really didn't know the people around her anymore. Maria had talked to her about this many times, but it was always the same answer: "Nobody bothers me."

"Mom, you have bars on your windows."

"So what? This neighborhood is safe. I feel *comfortable* here. Nobody bothers me."

My God, Maria would often think to herself, it's no wonder she likes that damn movie so much. There are crazy Italian women in it who think their kids are trying to take their houses from them. Even though her mother said she felt comfortable there – "as long as nobody bothers me" – the location of their home was never *completely* worry-free, even when Maria was growing up there. But her mother was who she was and wasn't about to change on a dime or anytime, actually. "Change" was not part of her vocabulary. She would often say that In Sicily people would often live their lives and die in the same house where they were born. Reminding her that they were not *in* Sicily, and that she was born here in the States never caused her to change her mind even just a little. "Nobody bothers me here."

So, harking back to one of her favorite quotes from Shakespeare about "discretion being the better part of valor," Maria decided not to bring the house up today. There were however a couple of other things she wanted to talk about as long as she was here. But first, they had to settle on dinner plans. It was no easy feat discussing *anything* with the two of them, but the sooner the meal was settled the better it would be.

"Hey, Mom, Aunt Elizabeth, I know a great place we can go for dinner. My treat."

The two sisters had been waiting for that statement, but, of course, they couldn't let it stand as it was.

"Well, all right, Maria. But you don't pay. We split it. You don't make no money in that damn job of yours."

A smile crossed Elizabeth's face as she snuck a look at Maria.

"We'll figure out the money, Ma, don't worry about it. And I know a real good place, but I got to talk to you about something first."

"I'm not moving. I'm comfortable here."

"It's not about moving, Ma. But you have a lot of stuff here. If you sorted it out, it would be easier to take care of this place. I mean, look at those chairs – chairs nobody sits in. Do you really need all those chairs? And what about all the things in your attic? It's like a museum up there. You're never gonna use *any* of those things. Why do you insist on keeping them?"

"Maria, you never know when you're gonna need them. And they're all in good condition."

Of course, what her mother neglected to say is that the reason so many of them are in such good condition is that a lot of them have never been opened. A prime example is a cell phone she bought twenty-five (yes, that's 25) years ago. It's still in the box it came in. Untouched, like a collector's item. But this idiosyncrasy is limited to things smaller than a breadbox. No sir. There are stories about cars that are hard to believe, unless, of course, if you know Marie.

For a long time, she had two cars. Two cars – one driver. When asked about the rationale for this, the lady's reply was simple and, to her, very logical: "What if my car breaks down? This way I have another one I can use." Maria begged and begged her mother to sell it, and she finally did. Well, it was actually Maria who sold it, though the process was so laborious and tortuous that it almost defied not only logic but reality. What should have taken a few days took weeks that seemed like years. "Put the price up high, you can always come down" was the strategy her mom advised. Miraculously, a boy from New York wanted it, and she haggled with him and his father for days over two hundred dollars – never mind that with maintenance and insurance she was wasting FAR more than that.

Most people have seen on TV the oft-used story about the little old lady whose car was in perfect condition because she kept it in the garage and drove it only to church on Sundays. Marie was one better than that. She bought a new car and hardly *ever* drove it at all – five years, less than 3,000 miles. Five years! When asked why she didn't drive it more, Marie evoked the same response she used when she had two cars: "What if it breaks down?" EWWWWWWW....the screech going through Maria's head could have competed with the shot heard round the world in intensity and duration. Competed? It would have won! Whenever the subject of change came up, whether it was a car, furniture, an appliance, or the house itself, Marie would put on the same "record" she had been playing for decades. It was always the same, and Maria pretty much knew it by heart. But it wasn't just the context that touched or aggravated the listener (depending on who was listening), it was the passion and emotion with which it was delivered that filled the air and everyone there with GUILT. Everyone, distant relative, neighbor, delivery man, or DAUGHTER. Once, in an ill-advised moment when she was much younger, Maria was about to say to her mother that if she could bottle and sell the guilt she was peddling the whole family could retire to a villa somewhere in the Adriatic and live there comfortably for the rest of their lives. Somehow, luckily, she had stopped herself after saying "Ma, if you could..." or this book would probably neverhave been even started, since Marie would still be sobbing her rebuttal. Maria often thought of that potential disaster when the "change" soliloquy was about to start.

"Maria, we've been here fifty years. You were a year old when we moved in. I raised three kids here. I know it's big and things have changed, but I'm comfortable here. Nobody bothers me. And I know I have a lot of stuff, but I keep it in case I need it. If I didn't keep those chairs, suppose someone comes over: where they gonna sit? It happened so many times. I throw something out, the next day I need it. So, if I don't throw it out, when I need it, I have it! And - I have this house. There were a lot of years, here, and a lot of people...."

There was no use getting into an argument over an attitude that wouldn't be changed without an act of God. Or perhaps even *with* an act of God, so Maria simply changed the subject.

"Ma, listen, I want you to stay here as long as you want to. As long as you feel comfortable. OK? Now, let's go out and get something good to eat."

Elizabeth gave a definitive nod, but Marie had a rather questioning look on her face, something Maria had seen all too often.

"What's the matter Ma? Why the frown?"

"What about my doctor next week. You gonna take me?"

"I said I would."

The conversation had taken a sharp turn, and Maria wanted to get off this road, and on the road, as soon as she could. She *always* took her mother to the doctor, and she *always* saw to her medicines and her general well-being. But none of this would be of any value if at least *some* guilt weren't thrown into the mix, so she figured she'd let her mom play a hand or two of "woe are Italian mothers," but not an entire game.

"Ma, you know you're my lady."

That usually did the trick, and it worked like a charm again.

"I know Maria, I know," she said with a warm smile. "I know."

That would have been the ideal time to turn their thoughts towards food and a place to get some, but there was something else which had to be addressed, and Maria reluctantly brought it up.

"Mom, just one more thing."

"Oh, no. Is it something bad? Is someone sick? Did someone die? You know, Linder has been very sick."

"Who?"

"My friend Linder. You know who she is."

Who the hell was she talking about? Was that a first name or a last name?

Elizabeth had just returned from the bathroom and caught the tail end of their discussion, and of course felt obligated to jump in.

"Marie, was she the daughter or the mother?"

"Who, Lindner?"

"Yes."

"She worked so hard she killed her mother. That's what she did. That's how much that Lindner cared about her mother."

Maria realized that there was no easy way out of this labyrinth her mother had led them into, but at least she figured out that the name – "Lindner" was really "Linda." But was she the mother or the daughter? It didn't really matter, because neither she nor her aunt or most probably her mom...knew who the hell she was. She quickly made a quick turn and steered the subject back to the doctor's appointment and away from "Lindner."

"OK, Mom, now don't forget to call me to double-check what time you want me to pick you up, all right?"

"For what, Maria?"

"For your doctor's appointment."

"You know that Lindner never took her mother to the doctor. She killed that poor old lady. Oh, and by the way I am having trouble using the phone you gave me I don't know my password."

"Ma, you don't need a password. But, if you're having trouble, you can just text me. You know how to text me, right?"

Her mom had a puzzled look on her face, and Maria at first thought she'd better back off, but the doctor's appointment was Wednesday, she had already taken the day, off, and if anything went wrong, it would most certainly turn out to be her fault. So, it was probably best to get it straightened out tonight. Her sanity depended on it.

"OK, Mom, now you have my phone number, right? But if it is easier, like I said, just text me. Or call me. Or don't do anything. I will be here Wednesday morning. All right?"

The puzzled look slowly changed into a smile.

"OK, Maria. I know you'll be here to get me. Thank you."

"Hey, Ma, you're my lady, right? Right! Let's go eat."

CHAPTER FOUR

Beware Of Greeks Running Diners....

They piled into Maria's car bound for "parts unknown," which was Mom's assessment of the trip, being that they hadn't really talked about where they were going to go to eat. But of course, there was a more immediate problem. Maria's car was a medium-sized Honda, perfect for going back and forth to Burns High School, but was also, according to her mom and aunt, the smallest car ever made in the hundred and twenty-five-year history of the internal combustion engine.

"You know Maria, this car might be OK for you when you're by yourself, but it got no room when you have somebody else in the car, don't you think? I can barely move. Tell that damn school to pay you more so you get bigger car."

Now, being Sicilian, Maria had some of the same blood coursing through her veins as her mother, and her aunt, for that matter. And at the moment it was starting to boil. She was about to ask her mother why it was that if the car had been good enough to take her to all her appointments at various doctors and agencies over the past five years, why wasn't it adequate enough for the three of them to take tonight? But if there was one thing she had learned over her many years teaching high school it was that sometimes you can't win. Taking a beat and cooling your jets often proves to be the best course of action, so she bit her already blistered tongue and just turned on the radio.

"I don't like this song, Maria. Most of these people just have one song. Not like Sinatra or Dean Martin. One song. And I don't like it anyway."

"Well, Mom, this is Bon Jovi. He's no one-hit wonder!"

"Oh, yeah, I know him. I know Stevie Wonder."

Maria just gently shook her head. You had to laugh, really, to keep at least some of your sanity. But it wasn't quite over.

"And where are we going for dinner?"

Her aunt had been quiet the whole time, and it startled Maria to hear someone speaking from the back seat.

"Yeah, I don't care about your car or your songs, but I am kind of hungry. Is this place close by?"

"We'll be there in about ten minutes, Aunt Elizabeth." Maria wished she were Elizabeth Montgomery so she could twitch her nose and be at their destination instantly, because she knew what was coming: 'the tapping' – as opposed to but just as disturbing as *The Shining*"! Both sisters had long, polished fingernails, which they used in a staccato-like cacophony of clicks upon the windows. And with every series of taps there appeared to be a recollection of some past catastrophe.

"Isn't that where Bill had that bad accident? Or was that Paul who had it?"

"Look at that car. That was the same car Lindner used to drive. isn't it? Didn't she crash it somewhere around here?"

The thoughts were totally random, and rarely, if ever, completed. Were these real events or just emotionally charged memories that actually never happened? Maria had long ago given up trying to figure out the answer to that question, and to hold onto what was left of her mental equanimity, she thought it best not to tackle it tonight.

She almost ran the red light, or perhaps it was red when she went through it, but no jury would have convicted her. They were there....!!

"We're here!" Maria exclaimed as she exhaled a day's worth of frustration.

They pulled into the parking lot of the Starling House Diner, which, from all appearances, looked like a good place to eat. The outside was framed by about a dozen tall and arching trees, and there were flowers and bushes in a beautiful arrangement which complimented the shiny and well lit edifice they were about to enter. There was a double parking lot, and it looked like they did a brisk business.

"This good place, Maria?"

"Would I take my mother and my aunt to a place that was no good? Would I? A lot of the teachers eat here."

Elizabeth cut to the chase, "As long as they have food and a bathroom, it's good enough for me. Let's go in!"

They walked up the short, sloping incline that led to the front door. A couple was just walking out, and they were saying how full they were and appeared to have a take home box with them They smiled and held the door for the three ladies.

"See that, Mom, they ate all they wanted and then had left overs to take home."

"Maybe they didn't like it and were just taking it out so they didn't have to eat it."

They went in, her mom and aunt talking and Maria just shaking her head.

The diner was crowded, but not jammed, and there seemed to be both booths and tables free in various locations.

"Now Maria, let's make sure we get a good place to sit. It's too cold right here; I can feel the air conditioner right on my head."

"Mother, we're standing at the entrance to the diner. They have to keep it cool; and don't worry, they won't make us sit on the floor."

They were greeted by a pleasant young man, about twenty five or so. He was clean shaven and neatly dressed in a pair of slacks and shirt. He could have been one of Maria's former students..

"Welcome, ladies. Would you like a booth or a table? We have both."

"Maybe a booth," Maria answered.

"Good idea, Maria. People can't kick the back of your chair when you're in a booth," Elizabeth chimed in.

"Yes, but we don't want one of those tight booths where you can't get in or out," said Marie. "Right, Liz?"

"Correct! And we don't want to be too close to the bathrooms. Phew! Sometimes the odor is too much."

"But we don't want to be too far away either, in case one of us has to go."

"Well said, Mare."

The young greeter, who seemed to have aged about ten years during his brief encounter with the sisters, stopped short right in the middle of the restaurant. He still had his smile, but as he glanced over his shoulder, he could see other people waiting to be seated, and he had to bring this to some sort of conclusion.

"Ladies, we stopped here so you could look around and find the perfect spot to enjoy your dinner."

Luckily, the "perfect spot" seemed to be right where they were standing. There was what appeared to be an adequately sized booth available, not close to – but not far from – the restrooms. However, there was still a problem: directly overhead was an air conditioning vent, and though it was really on the quiet side, and it wasn't particularly cold, the two ladies reacted as if they had been dumped in northern Alaska in December with a Texas tornado imported to circulate the freezing air.

"Oh, no, that air is coming right down on my head. It's freezing. Can't we sit somewhere else?" Marie exclaimed.

The host noticed the foursome near the door just getting up. He suggested that spot as an alternative.

"No, no, not there either. There is always a terrible draft when you sit near the entrance. Am I right, Liz."

"Yes, Mare. We can't eat with the wind blowing on us."

The young man spotted another couple about to leave what looked like a potential eating place, but the sisters had already spotted it and were shaking their heads. Marie started to cough.

"Oh, Liz, I can smell the food from here," quipped Marie, as she started to cough. "If we go closer to the kitchen, it will kill me; it's no good for my cough." Elizabeth nodded in solemn agreement.

Somehow, miraculously, they managed to find a booth. It wasn't a "perfect" place, but apparently it would do. The two sisters were nodding in acquiescence and Maria suppressed a scream. She told herself that she should be used to this because it happened every time – but no matter how many times you bang your shin, the pain is still there. And tonight had all the makings of one of their signature performances!

As the two sisters settled into their seats, their heads were swiveling as they took in the immediate surroundings, perhaps looking to see if some other negative feature may have been surreptitiously planted to spoil the ambiance Maria pulled the young man aside.

"My companions are my mother and my aunt. Do you know who our waiter will be?"

"It's probably going to be my father, the owner. We're a bit short tonight, and he likes to pitch in and meet his customers at the same time. Why?"

"Well, I usually talk directly to the waiter, but maybe you can tell him for me. I love these ladies, but they can be – how should I put it – a bit uh..."

"Eccentric?" the young man volunteered.

"Crazy!" Maria responded. "It will take them quite a while to decide on their selection, and I usually make it up to the waiter dollar-wise. Get it?"

"Got it! I'll tell my dad, but I think he'll be OK!" He then turned to the sisters. "Here are your menus, ladies. Your waiter will be here momentarily. Enjoy your dinner."

Marie and Elizabeth were just beginning to scan their menus when another gentleman appeared. He was about fifty, swarthy and dignified looking, with a mustache and casually but neatly dressed.

"Good evening, ladies. My name is Stavros, and it will be my pleasure to wait on you tonight. Actually, my wife and I own this place, but we're a little short of help, so I'm doing a little of this, a little of that. If there's anything you need, just let me know. I see you have your menus; would you like a little time to look them over?"

Raising her eyebrows just a bit, Maria answered, "yeah, that might be best."

Stavros gave an understated nod indicating he had been given a scouting report by his son. "Just let me know when you are ready," he uttered politely as he walked away a step or two.

"Well, Stavros, huh. Must be Greek with a name like that."

"Ma, you know as well as I do that every diner in Jersey is owned by a Greek."

"I was just making conversation. They usually have pretty good food, but you gotta watch them. You know what I mean, Maria? Although this one did seem nice. He did seem nice."

"Yeah, Ma, he did. But could we get back to your dinner selection?" Maria uttered desperately.

"My goodness, there are so many things to choose from!

What are you gonna have, Liz?"

"I don't know," her sister replied. "It's such a hard choice."

"Why don't we ask the waiter what he recommends," Marie suggested. "Hey, Stavros, come here," she shouted as she pointed to the owner.

Stavros, was at that moment was balancing a tray full of food for the table across the aisle. He nodded to indicate he would be right over – and he was.

"Well, are we all set?"

"Uh, not quite," Maria deadpanned.

"We thought you could suggest something," Liz replied hopefully.. "You have so much on the menu!"

"OK, what are you in the mood for? How about roast beef?"

"No, that repeats on me," Marie responded, putting her hand to her stomach. "And I don't like to see the blood.... eww...." as she moved her hand to cover her eyes.

"Our chicken is tasty and easy on the stomach," was Stavros' next suggestion.

"No, I had chicken this week," was Liz's counter.

Of course Maria had been through this all too many times – in fact, it was the same show *every time* they went out to eat. She marveled at the restraint that Stavros was showing.

Meantime, Elizabeth had to use the ladies room, so she told Maria to just get her a cup of minestrone and a grilled cheese and tomato sandwich. .

In the middle of the great dinner decision, Stavros seemed to get somewhat of a quizzical look on his face, and what followed was typical of a Greek and predictable of Marie – at least that's the way Maria felt!

"Excuse me if this seems forward, but are you two sisters? You are both so lovely and look so much alike."

Maria couldn't help laughing and shaking her head – the goddamn Greeks are all alike, she thought almost out loud.

Her mother, on the other hand, ate the hyperbole up, as she played one of her hole cards, a demur and flirtatious blush that enveloped her whole countenance.

"Oh, aren't you sweet? This is my daughter. But what a nice thing to say."

"Oh, I am sorry. But I can see where her good looks come from!"

"Well, if you say so!! You;re not so bad yourself!"

Stavros just nodded slightly as an acknowledgement. Maria was exercising all the self control she could muster as she matter of factly asked her mother if they could just order. So she did, both for herself and her aunt, who had not yet returned. Now it was center stage for mom, something that would always prove to be humorous and memorable, yet at the same time reminiscent of a TV sitcom..

"OK, hon, give me the matzo ball soup, but not too much chicken.and Yeah" – Her mother continued while looking downward at the imaginary soup – "Do you have any crackers?" Marie remained animated this whole time, as she then began to simulate breaking crackers up in the bowl of soup. Stavros was doing his best to suppress a grin, and Maria was just shaking her head with a gentle smile, as she quietly and matter-of-factly ordered lentil soup and a salad for yourself. But her Mom wasn't quite done.

"Oh, and hon, I like lots of butter. Make sure you bring the butter. Oh, and yeah, make sure you bring the crackers, too."

"Your wish is my command, fair lady," said Stavros, with such a genuine demeanor that even Maria was impressed. He took the menus with a flourish and promised to be right back with the soups.

"What a sweet man, Greek or no Greek."

"You're impossible, mother. Just awful!"

"Hey, the man knows a beautiful woman...excuse me... women...when he sees them."

Stavros was as good as his word, and was back in a flash with the minestrone, matzo balls, and lentils. Quite a trifecta..

"Do you want me to keep the minestrone hot till the other lady gets back?"

"You are soooo thoughtful, Stavros. *She* is my sister, and she'll be back in a minute. You can just leave it."

"All right, call me if you need anything else before the main course is ready, the owner offered as he walked away.

Marie had already begun to attack her soup, as she put the spoon into it and twirled around all the chicken pieces she really didn't want..

"They never get this right. Too much chicken, and not enough crackers! They're so cheap. What's the matter with that guy Stavros, or whatever his name is. He must be a new owner."

Maria finally had to say something...."Hey Mom, if they were CHEAP, wouldn't they be cheap with the chicken, and not with the crackers? Huh? Hold on; I'll get you some more."

"No one needs to order for me," her mother shouted, as she pointed toward Stavros with a gesture that would have made General Patton blush. She caught his eye almost literally – "Sir, sir, I want some more crackers."

Maria had this battle with her mother time and time again, but to no avail.

"Mom, haven't I told you that pointing is rude and aggressive body language?"

"Say what you want, but I know what I have to do," her mother stated triumphantly as the owner promptly arrived with an overflowing basket of crackers..

Stavros and the crackers arrived at the same time as Elizabeth, and as she scooted in to sit down she called Maria by name when asking if she could move just a little bit. Maria had inadvertently left a small Burns High School pad in her purse as she had packed her stuff in the hustle to leave her mother's house, and it fell out as she moved. It caught Stavros' attention.

"Excuse me for interrupting your dinner, ladies, but is that a Burns High School insignia?"

Maria nodded.

"And your name is Maria?"

Maria nodded again. This was getting interesting, especially for her mother, who took time out from "crackering" her soup to look up with a very intense grimace on her face.

"Then you must be *the* Maria. The Maria that teaches English and works with Nick.! So glad to meet you! I've heard so much about you, and here you are in person. You teach with Nick, right? He told me you were very smart – and very beautiful."

"Efharisto," Maria answered in her best Greek.

"You speak Greek so well. But Nick said you were."

"SICILIAN," her mother shouted.

Stavros didn't miss a beat.

"Hey, Greeks, Sicilians….it's all good!" Stavros laughed with a genuine tone that made it hard not to like the guy. Hard, but not impossible.

Stavros was still chuckling. "You're probably wondering how I know all these things. Well, Nick and I go way back. He used to work here with Mario when they were writing musicals. . So when he got a new writing partner, he told me all about you. Oh, and your money is no good here tonight. Enjoy!" Stavros walked over to his son and was still smiling as he apparently was filling him in on their newly found celebrity.

Maria's mother turned toward her with a reproachful look that could only mean an ill wind was blowing and about to turn in her direction.

"So, you have a writing partner? His name is Nick? It seems that everyone but your mother knows about it. Who is this 'Nick'? Nick what? And what are you writing?"

She turned to her sister.

"See, strangers know more about your kids' lives than their mothers. Just like in *MARTY.*"

Elizabeth nodded so hard her head almost hit the table. Luckily they were in a booth or she probably would have rocked herself out of the diner.

"Ma, I told you about him. You just didn't remember. Nick. Nick Pappas."

"Pappas? Pappas? He's a damn Greek, too?. Believe me, I would remember that. And he works with you?"

"Yes, we have lunch duty together."

"What is that, lunch duty?"

"Well, we watch the kids while they eat lunch."

"Where you watch them from?"

"Well, we sit at a table. That's how we got started writing the book. We have a lot of the same ideas."

"You can bet he's got ideas, and they got nothing to do with the book. You saw this guy, this Stavros, when we came in. They're all like that. They're all after one thing."

"But you didn't get mad when Stavros gave you a compliment!"

"That's different, I will never see him again. Ever. You see this guy every day! And he sits next to you! He knows you're married?"

"He knows. He's married, too. And he has lots of kids."

"See!!, They can't keep their hands off women."

"He ever tells you that you look nice? He told this Stavros guy that you are beautiful."

"It's just a compliment, Ma. That's all. You know what, he took piano lessons on our street."

"Our street? Where the house is?"

"It was many years ago, Mom."

"Mmmmmm," was all her mother uttered with her mouth,

but the wink and the shaking of her head and finger said it all.

"He's not a bad guy, Ma."

"Yeah, well, now that he knows, I bet he still drives by. Just watch your step. And don't wear any more dresses to that 'lunch duty,' you hear me?"

The "tennis match" between Maria and Marie was thankfully interrupted by the main course, brought by the apparently always smiling Stavros.

"Enjoy. And just call me if there's anything else you need."

When Elizabeth saw what her sister was having, she was beside herself.

"Oh, no, I didn't know you could order French toast!"

CHAPTER FIVE

Lunch Duty ...

Nick got to lunch duty first, so he settled in at the table occupied by the lunch duty teachers and yelled at a few kids just to keep his timing. The room was huge and had been constructed only ten years before when the school had undergone massive – and expensive – renovations. Several doors opened to the outside, which featured some picnic tables and a glorious view of the teachers' parking lot. The teachers' lunch room was at the far end and was a separate facility unto itself. It was a pleasant enough and spacious area in which to eat, but very few of the seventy odd teachers actually ate their lunch there since it was almost in a different zip code from the rest of the school. Some staff members would come by to grab a sandwich, but they would usually go back to their rooms to eat, so it was basically just Nick and Maria as far as teachers went. Speaking of Maria, where was she? Something must be up, Nick thought, and it was, as Maria came in with that all too familiar look on her face that meant he'd better tread lightly. She slammed her pile of stuff down on the table and uttered one of her infamous "ehhhh" sighs that could mean any number of things, but the bottom line was that she had something on her mind, and it wasn't the agenda for today's faculty meeting.

She turned and stared at Nick with a look that would have made Medusa envious. He said a quick silent prayer that her wrath wasn't directed at him. It wasn't.

"I just got a call from my mother. She was so proud of herself that she was able to get through"

"Well, that's good right? You had said she was having a problem with her phone."

"Yeah, but I was probably better off when she couldn't get me."

Nick knew that he shouldn't ask what he was about to, but he wanted it to look like he cared – which he did. How could he put this so it didn't look like he was prying, and at the same time not appear his query was just perfunctory.

"Maria, what's up?"

His partner was shocked at the directness and simplicity of his question. Usually, if ten words were adequate, Nick would use a hundred. But this time he would have put a mime to shame.

"Silent Cal would be proud, Nick.

"Huh?" replied the dumbfounded Greek. Perhaps just "dumb" would have been enough. "What?"

Aggravated as she was, Maria could not suppress a laugh.

"Usually you go on and on and on. You got right to the point, just as Coolidge used to do. I'm proud of you."

Nick sighed a big "whew" under his breath. He really liked Maria, but he was also just a bit – actually quite a bit – afraid of her, and she was one person you did not want to get mad at you. But it looked as if the storm clouds were receding a little..

She turned to face him, which was good unless she were yelling because her eyes were something else.

"Didn't mean to blow a gasket. It's just frustrating dealing with my mother. I told you I was taking a day Wednesday so I can take her to the doctor, right?" She didn't wait for an answer.

"So I told her to call me if there was a problem about anything."

Thinking that she was going to keep on rolling, Nick was caught flatfooted, and managed just a half uttered "So...?."

"So – she calls me this morning just as my class is starting, and like an idiot, I think It's an emergency and answer the damn phone. Guess what? She just wanted to talk. I've been teaching thirty years and my mother still can't get it through her head that I can't just put things on hold to listen to her day. Geees..."

"Been there, still doing that," Nick exclaimed. "They don't understand what we do or what the constraints are when we are in front of a class."

They high-fived!

"Oh, and by the way, Nick."

Nick broke out in a big grin.

"I knew there had to be a 'by the way' in here somewhere," he chuckled, quoting one of their favorite Jackie Gleason lines from THE HONEYMOONERS, a show both of them loved. The two of them started laughing so hard they were getting quizzical looks from several of the students passing by, as well as from the principal, who always bought his lunch during this period.

But for once Nick was ready, as he looked up with a grin and said..."Yeah, Mr. Morgan; we're working on a really funny part of the curriculum."

The head man just shook his head and kept on walking. Nick had had his share of battles with him, and so had Maria, but this looked like just another puzzle Morgan would have to leave in the box.

"Now, 'dear,' what were you going to tell me?" Nick inquired, still laughing uncontrollably.

"Not a big deal...I promised Stavros I'd tell you Hi."

"Stavros? Oh, Stavros at the diner! Did you eat there over the weekend?"

"No – I ran into this random guy on the street and asked him if his name happened to be Stavros. He said yes and so then I asked him if he knew you. And he said to say 'Hi.'"

Nick had been caught flat-footed...again.

"Of course I went to the diner, you idiot."

He could never keep up with Maria, so he just bowed his head in defeat.

"Nice place, huh, Maria?"

"Nice if you're going by yourself or with normal people. A trip to hell if you're going with your mother and your aunt. And, my lunch duty colleague, what exactly did you tell him about me?? Hmmm??"

"I told him that we were working together on a book about all our years teaching."

"And?"

"And that you were very bright."

Maria kept the glare on full.

"And, well, that you were easy on the eyes....actually, I think I used the word 'beautiful.' Was there a problem?" he asked with trepidation and a cringe embedded in his face.

"Well, not really a 'problem,' more like a hornet's nest. My mother found out we were working together, and that you used to take piano on our street....and that you're Greek At the very least she thinks you are stalking me; I'll stop there."

"Sorry, Maria."

"Well, for once it's not really your fault. Let me ask you a question: is your mother like that?"

"Not only my mother, but my aunt as well. Ironically, they are about seven years apart, and my Aunt Mable is the older one. Pretty close to your situation. And let me tell you something: from all the stories you've told me, they could be the same people."

Nick was getting somewhat of a glazed look over his eyes, as he started to daydream and talk through his thoughts. "Yeah, it sounds as if they're pretty much the same people. Not easy to deal with as they're getting older – or ever. You should have experienced what it was like growing up with the two of them shadowing my every move. I'm lucky I made it this far."

"My aunt is a past master at jokes, especially at someone else's expense. Not to mention guilt trips. Oh, Lord, I could tell you some stories about her!"

"And your mother?"

"Don't get me started," Nick replied. "They are both good at what they do, which was to get you to do what they wanted you to do, but their styles are completely different. Mable would come with a Sunday punch, sort of like your mom, while my mother would wear you out with her footwork and then jab you into submission. And they're still going strong. My mom has tucked away grudges and guilt for decades – literally. I could tell you stories that would make you cringe.

Just then the fire alarm rang, and they had to herd two hundred students out into the parking lot.

"I'll take a rain check on those stories, Greek," Maria exclaimed as Nick was busy clearing out some reluctant seniors, who apparently felt that the school rules no longer applied to them.

"You got it Maria. Hey, you know what, this might make a good book. I mean a second book, all about our moms and aunts. Whadayathink?"

Before she could answer the principal re-appeared, vigorously waving his hand in a rapid circular motion to indicate they needed to get the kids out quicker. Nick was about to say something when Maria shot him a deadly reprimand with her now blazing eyes.

She was right. Nick buried his comment inside - expletives not deleted.

CHAPTER SIX

"Is That Asking Too Much?

Nick was on his way home from school and decided to stop at his mother's to see how things were and to see if perhaps she needed something at the store. He tried to stop there once a week just to check in on her, and he would call her every couple of days just to be sure she was doing OK. Of course, she wanted him to call her every day, but he had decided long ago that would not be a good idea. He needed a bit of space between them, and besides, if he had gotten in the habit of calling every day, a missed day would be cause for concern – and guilt.

She was glad to see him and had the grocery list all ready. "When do you need the stuff, Ma?"

"No rush, a day or two would be fine. Just be sure to get everything I want, and be sure you buy the brands and sizes I indicated. OK?"

Of all the regular "duties" Nick had to do, going food shopping for his mother headed the list when it came to stress. He was used to buying large sizes for his own family, and for the most part, one brand was as good as another. His mother was

40

finicky when it came to *everything,* but there had to be an asterisk next to food shopping because she was the most precise and had zero tolerance when it came to her food supplies. Nick looked at the list: about fourteen items. It would have taken him about twenty minutes at the outside to shop and get checked out if he were doing his own shopping. But this was different. It took him about twenty minutes just to go over the damn list, and he could feel the stress as he looked over the things once he had gotten back into his car. Nothing out of the ordinary, just the usual stuff: tuna fish, peanut butter, bread, eggs, cream cheese. A grown man really should not be scared of a shopping list, but just looking at it brought out a bevy of fears and pressures.

Of course, Nick had two strikes against him. First of all, the supermarket near his mother's house was not the one he usually shopped at. And there was no real order to the list he was intently looking at. Nick's lists, which were actually just visualizations, had the items in close proximity to each other in the store and also near each other on his "list." He wasn't sure how his mother's shopping list was put together, but if he ever got the wrong thing, or worse yet, forgot one, there would be more than hell to pay.

Nick pulled up to the store, grabbed his jacket and his keys, and strode in, mumbling a thing or two which cannot be printed here. He tried to give himself a pep talk, but his heart wasn't in it. So he settled on just taking one item at a time and getting it right. If it took two hours, so be it. Of course, it would have helped had he not left the damn list in the car! His loud and clear "goddamnit" resonated across the parking lot as he marched out to his small SUV. He uttered one more expletive as he unlocked the vehicle, grabbed the paper, and then slammed the door so hard it sounded like a shot, causing the guy in the next parking space to nearly jump out of his seat. After flashing the man the dirtiest of looks, Nick headed back into the store, determined to get out before it got dark.

Meanwhile, in another galaxy....just a few miles away.....
"Mom, what is it you want me to get you? I never seem to buy the right thing. What is the problem?"

"If you paid attention to what I was saying, we wouldn't have to have this conversation every time you go shopping. It's the least you could do for me. I gave birth to you, you know. Without me, there would be no you. Did I ever tell you that?"

"Only a few thousand times, only a few thousand times."

"There's no need to get fresh. Someday you will miss me and be sorry you didn't treat me better. Now, are you listening?"

"Yes, Ma, I'm listening. Go ahead."

"OK, it's actually very simple, Maria. I just need you to get me some food. It shouldn't be that hard. I don't eat that much. Is that asking too much?"

Maria took a breath. She and her mother had this same conversation many times before, and there was no use getting aggravated. It was just the way things were, so she put on her game face, paused, and as calmly as she could, answered in very measured tones.

"I always do your shopping for you. Just tell me what you need."

"My cereal, I need my cereal. It isn't that heavy. And you know what else I eat, right? You can get everything I need. But don't go getting those store brands. They are terrible. And you know my arm hurts. I can't really pick things up very well."

Despite her practice over the years, Maria couldn't help a slight grimace as she cringed a bit to keep from losing her temper. It was tough enough going shopping when she had a list. The line "you know what else I need" was a lose-lose situation. And sometimes the store brands were the only ones that fit what was needed. Good Lord. Her mother noticed the slight change in her daughter's demeanor, and, of course, had to make a comment.

"What's the matter, Maria, why are you so fresh to me? Just like everybody else. My friend hasn't called me in days. He doesn't care if I'm dead or alive. I think he's bipolar or something. He doesn't even want to see if I'm still alive. He's got some kind of mental condition."

"Ma, listen. He'll call. He always does. And he cares about you. If someone doesn't touch base with you every thirty seconds you think they've forgotten you. Just like with me. I call and come over as often as I can. And he's not bipolar!"

"Maria, why do you always take everyone else's side against your mother? Can't you agree with me one time? Just once I'd like to hear you say: 'Yeah, Mom, you're right, I know just what you mean.' Couldn't you do that, just one time? Did you hear me?"

There was really nothing her dutiful daughter could say that would have appeased her mother when she went in that direction, so Maria basically threw in the towel with a subdued "Yes, Ma, yes." But her mom was not quite finished.

"Can they deliver the food? Make sure you don't get the store brands. Did I ever tell you about Linder? She used to live around the corner from us. There's a story on every corner. Every corner. What happened to her?"

At just about the same time, Nick was going up and down the aisles in the food store trying to find the particular deodorant – brand and size – that his mother wanted. There must have been a hundred different smell protectors, as he often called them, but not the one she wanted. Wait, was that it, buried among the travel choices, all about thumbnail size?

Nick grabbed it and looked at the specifications which he could barely read. : It was two ounces more than what his mother had indicated. Well, close enough for government work as he used to say in high school. He grabbed the Secret, threw it in his cart, and started for the registers. He counted the items, fourteen, then double-checked the number on the list – fifteen. How was that possible? He did a quick inventory – Where the hell was the tuna fish? He knew he had gotten it because it had taken him a good ten minutes to get the right brand and number of ounces.

He could have sworn, which is what he did, that he had gotten it and put it in his cart. And he was right, he had, but he also had put it in the collapsible "shelf" in the front, the one with the big gaps that things could easily fall through, including, apparently, the ultra-small can of tuna. The canned fish aisle was at the far end of the store, but as he started back, he caught a glimpse of a shopping cart whose user was looking for something a few feet away. There, in the center of her cart, was another can of the elusive fish. He felt like a pickpocket as he grabbed it and headed for checkout...never a dull moment when dealing with his mother – and himself!

CHAPTER SEVEN

The Plane To Perdition

Newark Airport

"American Airlines flight non-stop to Los Angeles now boarding for first class passengers at Gate 11."

The two sisters had been at the airport for hours, and the call for their plane seemed almost too good to believe.

"Let's go, Mare. That's us." They had checked their bags earlier, but they seemed to have a whole storefront of carry-ons. Somehow they managed to get everything in hand, including their purses, which were big enough to hold a body and contained just about everything else. They made their way through – literally – swarms of people on their way to and from the planes. Had they been a bit younger NFL scouts would have been keeping an eye on them.

"Oh, excuse me, sir," Elizabeth apologized as a well-dressed businessman and his coffee went flying.

"Why you say you're sorry? That man stepped right in front of you?" her sister admonished her.

"I was just trying to be polite."

"You're too nice, Liz. Come on, we're going to miss our plane."

They were actually just a few steps away from the gate for their plane, but by the length of the line, it wouldn't be leaving anytime soon. The sisters plopped their bags down, and it was then that they realized how many people were ahead of them.

"We're gonna be here all morning, Liz."

"We've already been here all morning," her sister replied, exasperated, aggravated, and exhausted. "I'm tired. You wanna just go home?"

"Go home? You know how hard my daughter works at her stinking job so she can send us on a vacation? We can rest on the plane. Look, the line is moving."

It was indeed moving, albeit rather slowly. Of course, the tickets had to be checked, as did the bags and passengers. It was a long, laborious process, and it seemed interminable to the two ladies. But, lo and behold, three couples had been checked through, and the sisters were within earshot of the entrance. And then all hell seemed to break loose, as the volume of an animated conversation between someone and an airline official reverberated throughout the terminal.

There were two women together and there seemed to be some problem with their tickets. One of them was short and dressed casually, and the other one was a bit younger and thinner, and very professional looking. She was dressed to the nines. They looked like they were in their mid to late sixties and from their appearance, they could have been sisters. In fact, they were sisters, and one of them was going at it with the harried airline official, who was doing her best to be courteous and still do her job.

The talkative lady turned to her sister, who was aghast with embarrassment.

"See, Marica, we wait all this time, and now we got to wait some more. It's cause they don't like what we look like. It's cause we're Greek! Just like when I was in sixth grade and they wanted me to clean up because I was an immigrant."

"They wanted you to clean up because it was a home economics class, and that's what you were supposed to do."

The "gatekeeper" had had enough.

"LADIES! You can settle your family squabbles on your own. I've got a ton of people to get on this plane, so I will have to ask you to leave and come back at the proper time. Is that clear?"

Meanwhile, the Sicilian sisters had been taking all of this in, and their disposition was turning sour in a hurry.

"Look at those two women, holding everything up. We've been in line forever, and now they are making it even longer. What is wrong with them?"

"I don't know, Mare. Some people have no consideration."

Just then the shorter of the two at the beginning of the line let loose with a a string of expletives in Greek, for which she was quickly berated by her sister.

"Mable, please. People are turning their heads."

"I don't care. We waited all this time. We're at the front of the line. We're next. It's our turn."

The airline employee took it all in stride, and in fact, broke out into a smile. Calmly, she addressed the two Greek sisters.

"Ladies, you can say whatever you want, in Greek or any other language. But the fact of the matter is, you're in the right place at the wrong time. Now, if you'll excuse me....Next."

Marica grabbed her sister by the elbow and the two of them headed back toward the seats, Mable cursing all the way.

The two Sicilians didn't miss a trick. Marie turned to her sister with an "I knew it" look on her face.

"Did you hear that, Liz? Greeks. Always causing trouble. I knew it, I knew it.

Just like that damn Greek that works with my daughter, that Pappas. Always breaking the rules, always after something!"

Liz nodded in acquiescence as they found themselves at the front of the line.

"Hello, ladies," said the relieved airline rep. "May I see your tickets?"

Marie and Elizabeth rummaged through their bags, and finally came out with their paperwork.

"Here, Liz, I'll give it to her," Marie offered. "Might as well try to make it easier for her cause she's had a rough time this morning with those damn Greeks."

Liz gave her paperwork to her sister, who couldn't resist a shot at the two previous sisters as she handed them to the woman behind the counter.

"I'll bet you are glad to be rid of those two. What a scene they made!"

The airline official couldn't resist a small smile as she looked at the tickets and handed them back.

"I'm sorry ladies. You're going to have to return in a bit. This line is for first class ticket holders only!"

CHAPTER EIGHT

Greeks and Sicilians

Marie and Liz managed to get back on the line when the call came over for the coach passengers, but the Greek duo was nowhere to be seen, and Marie was hoping they were on some other plane, or no other plane, or had gone home. She was not one to forgive and forget, but as she boarded the plane her thoughts did manage to turn back to the trip and their means of conveyance. She was not fond of flying, and neither was Elizabeth, a feeling attested to by the appearance of their rosary beads before they even entered the airplane. The flight attendant at the door nodded knowingly as the two ladies, their bags, and their beads paraded by.

"Aisle 14, seats A and B, ladies. Enjoy the flight," she said warmly.

The two sisters made their way toward their seats, reading the number of each row as they passed it. They finally reached their destination, and now the question became where to put their carry-ons and who was going to get which seat. There was a whole line of passengers behind them of, course, all waiting impatiently to get themselves settled. But they seemed to be oblivious to the plight of their fellow travelers as they debated who and what would go where.

"You wanna sit by a window, Mare? I know you like to see outside. Oh, this bag doesn't fit here What we gonna do?"

"Why don't you sit near the window, Liz. I just sit in the middle. It's OK."

"OK, thanks, Mare," Liz replied, relieved that the seats had been worked out. Of course, there were a couple of hitches to be resolved.

"But wait, Mare, what if someone sits next to you that you don't like?"

"Don't worry. I just turn and talk to you. It's OK."

Elizabeth still had a rather large bag on her lap in addition to her purse, but her sister sat down before that situation was settled, Of course, Marie had a bag and purse of her own. The ladies and their "luggage," all piled into two seats were quite a sight. It made stuffing a phone booth from the Twenties seem like a walk in the park.

Not to worry, though; Marie appeared to have an easy solution.

"Here, Liz, give me your stuff. I'll put it on the seat next to me. I got my stuff there. We'll just put them all on the seat. It looks like no one's sitting there, and the plane is almost full.."

Marie was correct with one of her conclusions. The plane was filling up, but the seat next to her was supposed to be occupied;but the passenger and her companion were late. Of course, the flight attendant wouldn't have allowed their belongings to stay on the seat, but she hadn't made her walk through yet, mostly because there seemed to be a bit of a rhubarb brewing near the door. Apparently, there were two late arriving passengers, and one of them was "fit to be tied," an expression she kept using over and over.

"If they had let us check in before, we would have already been on the plane," she said to her companion, who was also her sister.

"It was our fault. That line was for first-class passengers. If you hadn't insisted on calling your daughter, we would have been sitting already," her flustered companion countered.

"Well, if they had any pay phones in this damn airport, we wouldn't have had to go searching all over the place."

"Mable, I told you that we wouldn't find any. Everybody has cell phones now."

"Well, good thing I asked that woman at the car rental place. Now I don't have to worry about Jo Ann. Now that I hear her voice."

"You told the woman it was an emergency."

"Marica, it was an emergency. We gonna be three thousand miles away. I just want to be sure she will be OK."

"She does have a husband, you know."

"That good-for-nothing George? He can't even take care of himself."

Luckily, the two Sicilian sisters had closed their eyes; they were vigorously working on their worry beads as they focused on the imminent liftoff of the plane. They were able to get a brief respite from their one-sided feud with the Greek sisters since they didn't hear or see the altercation just a few feet away. But that was about to change! The flight attendant, who had been the same one taking the tickets just a short time before, had long since run out of patience.

"Ladies, could you take your family squabble to your seats, please? We will be taking off shortly, and there are several things the crew needs to do to prepare. Please come in and enjoy your flight...or fight. as the case may be."

"Ella, Melpo," the younger one pleaded. "Come on."

Mable did come on, though it took them a while to walk to their seats, since she stopped every step to berate the phone company, the airlines, and mostly her son-in-law. It took them a good five minutes to walk about forty feet, which was probably fortunate since the sound of the air fan and the engines warming up had put the two Sicilian sisters on the edge of the land of nod. They actually looked like a couple of kittens curled up in a basket, as Marie's head was resting on her sister's shoulder.

The Greeks finally arrived at their seats, only to find Marie's and Liz's luggage piled in a heap. Luckily one of the crew was just returning from the men's room, and before Mable could raise a big fuss, he threw them up into the overhead compartments along with the bags Mable and Marica had on them. As often happens, Marie's doze incorporated what was actually going on into her dream, and she poked her sister to wake her up.

"Liz, Liz, the Greeks stole our bags. The Greeks stole our bags!"

She turned toward the aisle only to see Mable sitting there, for once just minding her own business. Of course, Mable knew nothing about the Sicilians' animosity toward her and her sister, or the supposed theft of luggage. She looked at Marie and was about to introduce herself when the flight attendant came walking by to do the seatbelt check.

"Ladies, we are about to take off. Please fasten your seatbelts."

The tension was broken a bit, as Liz and Marie got them on easily, but Mable's was all twisted and gnarled, and she was starting to fume. Marie laughed good-naturedly as she offered to help. Her fellow passenger accepted her offer quite readily.

"Thank you so much. Bad enough my sister makes me wear the damn things in her car. She drives so slow that even if we hit something nothing would happen. My name is Mable."

Almost against her will, Marie began to warm up to this lady, nationality notwithstanding. She did seem friendly and down to earth, and it would be a long flight Might as well make friends. Besides, there was something about her that seemed to resonate with the Sicilian. It would turn out that there were quite a few things they had in common.

"You know, whoever is running this airline should be locked up – the way they treat their passengers," Mable began out of the blue. "You know my sister and I got all the way to the front of the line, and then they kicked us out. Just because we don't got first-class seats. We waited all that time. It would have killed them to let us come onto the damn plane?"

Marie broke into a big belly laugh.

"So that's what happened to the two of you? That's why you were yelling at them?"

"Yeah, and my sister, over there(she points across the aisle)...she gets all mad cause I raise my voice. They're lucky I didn't take off my shoe and smack that woman in the head."

"I know what you mean. The same thing happened to us. They waited till we were all the way in the front, and then they tell us. Terrible."

"I think maybe they don't like Mediterranean people," Liz added. "My name is Liz, by the way. Pleased to meet you."

"Endaxi," Mable replied in Greek. "I said that to my sister, and she got all upset. I know when people don't like me. I'll have you know we're from Cephalonia, the biggest island in the Ionian Sea. Where you from?"

"Well," Marie answered. "We're from an even bigger is-land – SICILY"

"Sicilians, Greeks....it's all good," Mable exulted.

A light went on in Marie's head. Where had she heard that before?

Just then another light went on, as the plane was ready for takeoff. A voice came over the speakers informing everyone to be sure their seats were in the upright position, their tables were secure, and their seat belts were on. The airliner began to taxi into position for takeoff. Mable glanced over at her sister, who was all set to go - of course. She smiled back at her to indicate that everything was OK on her side of the plane. An odd couple if there ever was one.

"My sister. She got mad at me cause I want to call Jo Ann to see if she is all right. Not my fault there's no more pay phones anywhere. I just want to be sure she is all right. We're gonna be gone a whole week to the other side of the country. What's so bad that I call her? I ask you?"

Marie was listening intently to Mable's narrative.

"Mable, who is Jo Ann?"

"Oh, she's my daughter. But . you know what Marica says – that's my sister's name - she says to me why I'm worried, she has a husband. Jo Ann, she means. Jo Ann has a husband. He will take care of her while we're gone. . Her husband, George. George the pushover and pain in the ass. He's gonna take care of her? George? Don't make me laugh. Only a mother knows. You have children, Marie? You love them but they break your heart. Why does she has to marry that idiot? His family's not even from Cephalonia. They're from near Sparta, somewhere. A mainland Greek. They're different. You have children?"

This woman could talk!! Marie could barely keep up with all the details and questions. But Mable wasn't finished by a long shot.

"All the damn Greeks in Washington Heights, she has to marry him! When she was going out with him he was always late. Always, you hear me? He doesn't have a damn watch to tell the time? I yell at him every time. You know what he does? He smiles. What kind of an idiot smiles at you when you yell at him? You'd think she would listen to her mother?"

By this time both Marie and Liz were captivated by Mable's rapid excoriation of her son-in-law.

"Did you tell her not to marry him?" Liz asked.

"Of course, what do you think? I tell her next time he comes for her I gonna lock the door. I wish I did. He ruined my hallway!"

"He did what?" Marie and Liz asked in unison.

"In those years, I lived in New York, in apartment. Fourth floor. There is a long hall leading to the other rooms, and I just had it painted. Not just painted, but stencil put on. You know how much that cost?"

Marica of course had heard this story many times and started to smile in anticipation.

"It's not funny!" Mable exclaimed as she shot a look at her sister. "I had a beautiful stencil put on the walls. See, the hall is not wide. And that damn George comes in carrying some packages with his elbow sticking out, and he erases the whole damn stencil all the way down the hall. I could have killed him. I told my daughter to break up with him right there. Does she listen? Of course not. And you want to know what he does? He starts laughing."

By this time Marie and Liz and Marica were all laughing, as were the people in the seats in front and back of the excited narrator. Almost on cue the engines suddenly picked up in intensity and the plane began to accelerate for takeoff. The Sicilians were laughing so hard they almost forgot about their worry beads, Marica had her hand over her eyes to cover the tears of laughter, and Mable just shook her head as she thought of George!

Everything went smoothly aeronautically, and soon they were at cruising speed and altitude. The pilot came on with the customary welcome and the flight attendants were seeing to the comfort of their charges. Mable broke the silence first. Shocker!

"So, you have children Marie?"

"Yeah. Three. My one daughter lives in California."

"Oh, so you going to go see her when we get out there and stay with her?"

"Ha! See her? Stay with her? She's not even gonna be around. I get a phone call just before we leave, and she tells me they are going away for a week or two. Did you hear me? A week or two! *Now* she has to go away? How often I get to California? Kids, they don't care about you at all. I mean, since my husband passed away, that's all I got. I give birth to them and they don't care if I live or die. I fly three thousand miles and they go away. It's awful to be old and be alone."

All the while Mable was nodding her head vigorously.

"I know, I know. We both widows, too, me and Marica. You kill yourself with worry and raise them and feed them and then they grow up and they don't care what you do. But I still worry. Then I try to call my daughter to see if everything is all right, and we almost miss the damn plane"

"I told my sister we should take the train. We could see something while we go out there – farms and cities and mountains. Now what do we see....clouds and sun and more clouds."

The other side of the plane chimed in.

"Mable, we went over all this. With the plane we're there in six hours, and we have more time to do things."

"My sister thinks she's so smart. Well, she is smart. But she's not always right." The "smart" sister just shook her head and went back to her magazine.

"I know what you mean," Marie exclaimed. "Just like my daughter. She's smart, too, but she's not as smart as she thinks she is. And she needs to treat me better."

Mable nodded her head. "I guess you're mad that she's not going to be there to see you."

"No, not that one. My other daughter, Maria. She teaches English in high school I think she read every book ever written, and she knows a lot of stuff. But she should still be considerate and treat me with respect. Don't you think?"

"Yeah, your daughter Maria sounds like my nephew. He's a pretty good guy, but sometimes he's too smart for his own good. I mean, he went to this fancy college, and he winds up being a teacher. He has a lot of kids and no money. Well, I gotta say this....he gave us this trip for a Christmas present. That was nice, I gotta admit."

"Hey, you know what's funny....that's why we're going to California. Maria gave this vacation to *us* as a Christmas present, too. And she paid for a cab to take us to the airport this morning. She got no money, either."

"I know, Marie. Those damn schools don't pay them shit," Mable exclaimed. Then the elder Greek started to chuckle and then segued into a rolling belly laugh.

"What's so funny, Mable?" Liz asked.

"I just thought of something! I think they gave us these trips just to get the hell rid of us!"

"You're right, you damn Greek!" Marie yelled out loud with a coast-to-coast smile. "You are so right!"

The three of them would have done the Three Stooges proud! Meanwhile, Marica, or Ricky, as most of her family called her, bore just a trace of a smile as she relaxed a bit with her eyes closed and her mind somewhere else as the plane streamed along with a quiet hum.

The two sisters could not have been any more different. They were both born in Cephalonia (which was, by the way, the largest Greek island in the Ionian Sea). They came to America as children with their mother and father. Marica was seven years younger, bright, and well educated. Her sister was not fond of school. People were her forte; she was outgoing and sociable and full of stories. When she would come out to visit from New York City out to Jersey, a forty-minute ride, she could relate the life history of just about everyone on the bus. She was also outspoken and not afraid to challenge anyone about anything. Just ask the flight attendant. It was little wonder that she and Marie hit it off.

"Hey, Marica," Mable called to her sister. "I want you to meet my friends. Wake up."

"I was just resting my eyes, I wasn't sleeping."

"Whatever," Mable observed. "Hey Marie, Liz, this is my sister, Marica. Very nice, very smart. I embarrass her all the time."

"Well, not *all* the time," came the quick response from the younger Greek. "Pleased to meet you, ladies."

There were smiles all around as the foursome got better acquainted.

"Your sister was telling us about her daughter and her son-in-law. He sounds like a character!"

"Yeah, I caught the destroy the wall story," Marica replied.

"Did that really happen?" Liz asked.

"What, you think I'm lying?" Mable scowled, with a big smile thrown in.

"No, no," Liz protested. "It just sounds like something from a movie or TV show."

"If they ever made a TV show about George they would call it *THE IDIOT..*"

Everyone laughed, and Marica felt obliged to come to the defense of both her sister and her beleaguered son-in-law. Still laughing, she assured their new Mediterranean acquaintances that the wall incident was indeed true.

"...and George, yes, he is somewhat of a character, but he has the sweetest disposition of anyone you'd ever want to meet. Can you imagine having my sister as your mother-in-law?"

But Mable wasn't quite finished with her son-in-law – actually, she would never be finished, but she was on a roll and she wasn't about to stop now.

"Listen, Marica, don't put it all on me. How about that time when he knocked all your figures off the speakers? I don't think you were so pleased with that, were you!"

Marica nodded her head back and forth and then broke into uncontrollable laughter, which was rare for her. She leaned across the aisle and directed her comments right at the

Sicilians so they could get the full effect of what she was about to say.

"So, ladies, it was Christmas Day, and George and Jo Ann came over for Christmas dinner. Now, try and picture this: when you come into my hall there is a large archway on the left into the living room. Book ending the entrance were two big, round speakers on the floor. My son had brought them home from when he was in the Army, and we had about six or seven porcelain Christmas decorations on each one."

Mable jumped in. "Also, you gotta know this: my sister's house is the cleanest spot on the face of the earth. Nothing is out of place. You could eat off the floor."

The younger sister gave Mable a quick dirty look.

"Well, it's true, Marica. Go ahead, finish."

"So George comes in with an armload of long Christmas presents, and as he turns to go into the living room, he knocks over all the knick-knacks on one of the speakers."

Everyone yelled "GEORGE!"

"And as he turns to see what he did, he knocks all the pieces off the other speaker." The Sicilians were crying they were laughing so hard, and Mable was doubled over in hysterics. Even Marica, who was shaking her head vigorously as she remembered George's "two-step," and couldn't keep the belly laughs away.

But the story wasn't quite over as Mable continued...

"And then, after everyone takes their coats off, my stupid son-in-law sits down on the couch and my sister brings him some hot egg nog. Now, in front of the couch is a marble table that must weigh two tons, and it's like new and my sister's pride and joy. There are at least six coasters right in front of that knucklehead George, and what does he do? He puts the HOT cup of egg nog right on the table. I thought Marica was gonna kill him!"

Liz was beside herself. "Listen, listen...my sister has a table just like that... marble with gold edging, right? Right?"

The Greek sisters nodded in unison.

Marie picked up the baton...."Yes, I do. And just last week, when my daughter Maria was over, she did the same thing, only with hot espresso coffee!"

"They have no regard for precious possessions," Marica stated matter of factly.! "And if you try to protect your things because they're valuable..."

"Or mean something to you," Marie threw in....

"Or BOTH!" Mable exploded.

"Then they say you're too fussy or too picky or just a pain in the ass!!" said Liz as she shook her head vigorously and rocked with a vengeance.

"Our kids have no idea how hard it is to keep beautiful things in good condition over many years. They're spoiled," added Mable.

"AMEN!!" echoed the "fearsome foursome" in unison!

Their unanimity was interrupted briefly by the flight attendant...

"Ladies and gentlemen, the movie for this flight will be starting in a little while. We have headsets for those of you who want to view it. I would recommend it, because it's funny and yet pretty true to life. It's a Steve Martin movie called *PARENTHOOD.*."

"Oh, I never see that one. How about you, Liz, you ever see that movie? You, Mable?"

The two ladies shook their heads to indicate that they had not.

"How about you, Marica, you ever see it?" Mable wondered.

"No, I haven't, but I like Steve Martin."

"*PARENTHOOD.* I bet it's about kids that don't listen to their parents, just like *MARTY,*" Marie observed emphatically.

Marica was quick to agree: "*MARTY,* now there's a great movie."

CHAPTER NINE

To Sleep... For Sure to Dream

The four ladies were looking forward to watching the movie and were getting comfortable both in their seats and in their conversations.

"So, Marie, you see this movie before?" Liz asked.

"No, but Maria was telling me about it. Mable, you ever see it?"

"No, but like you said, Steve Martin is funny. He was good in *CHEAPER BY THE DOZEN,*" Mable answered.

"How about *SATURDAY NIGHT LIVE?*" Marica's voice bounced across from her solitary seat. "He was so funny in that!"

"Yeah, yeah," Marie echoed. "I loved that bit he did with Belushi about the Greeks owning the diner!"

"No Coke, Peksi. Czeeseburger, Czeeseburger," Liz chimed in.

Mable was doubled over laughing.

"They sure had the accent down good, especially not being Greek!"

As the credits started to roll, the eyes of the four women started to slowly fade, and soon they were all either asleep or in that twilight stage where you're half and half. Of course, Hamlet was right on the money when he said "to sleep perchance to dream...," because they did both as the film provided some sound sleeping background and the plane wound its way across the country....

Union, NJ – Ten Years Earlier....

"Hi, Aunt Mable, when did you get here? I didn't know you were coming out. Did you walk here all the way from the bus stop?"

"No, your father picked me up. I called him yesterday. I guess he didn't tell you? Well, whatever. I thought I'd stay a couple days and give your old man a break from cooking. Where's your brother?"

Mable was talking to her niece, a senior in high school. She had a brother who was a junior in college, and they, along with their widowed father, lived in a modest but comfortable home in a suburb about twenty-five miles from New York. Mable would come out to visit every so often, usually staying with Marica, who lived only a few blocks away. But this time she decided to stay with her brother-in-law and his two kids.

No matter where she was, Mable would assess the situation and take charge, especially where family was concerned.

"So, where's your brother?"

"He's got a rehearsal with his wedding band." Her brother, John, was a very talented singer and trumpet player. He was going to college but had a band as a sideline. They played for weddings and proms and parties. And they were good.

Just then Cathy sneezed, and she wiped her eyes, which were beginning to run a bit.

"You better take care of that cold!" Mable warned her. "It could develop into something worse, and you don't want to be sick your senior year."

Cathy assured her aunt that it wasn't anything to worry about and that it was mostly allergies anyway. They were about to go toe to toe on this when luckily the doorbell rang. It was Tony, a friend of her brother's. He and John had been good friends since grammar school, and he was almost like a member of the family. Mable had a bit of a scowl cross her face when she saw who it was because she didn't want her niece to get too "friendly" with him. He was a good guy and really very nice, but he wasn't in college and that was a no-no as far as Mable was concerned. He was on his way to work at the garage and just wanted to drop off a book he had borrowed, so it was a quick hello and goodbye. But Mable had to get a shot in any way.

"You know, your father told me that he doesn't work on the car engines, just the outside of the cars," she threw at her niece.

"Aunt Mable, I'm not gonna marry him; we're just friends," Cathy answered, as she put on a jacket.

"Where are you going?"

"To Nick's game."

Her cousin was a high school baseball coach, and they had a state tournament game just a few miles away.

"Are you crazy? With that cold you have? You see how cool it is out. You're gonna get pneumonia!"

"Aunt Mable, this jacket is warm. I'll be fine."

"And I'm telling you not to go. If you go I hope I get hit by a bus!"

As she tossed and turned in her sleep, Mable grabbed a hold of Marie by the arm and shouted loud enough for the stewardess to come check to see if everything was OK.

"I hope I get hit by a bus."

With a smile the attendant assured Mable and the now awake and startled Marie that there was no chance of that happening while they were in the air.

The quizzical look on Marie's face warranted an explanation and her new traveling companion told her all about the incident with her niece, who did NOT go to the game.

Marie nodded vigorously and patted Mable on her knee several times.

"I know just what you mean, Mable. I know just what you mean!"

"And she had a liking for that friend of her brother's – she wasn't fooling me. I mean, he's not a bad kid, but he's no genius either. He'll probably have to work for someone else his whole life. He doesn't have the brains to go to college or the spunk to be his own boss someday. You know?" She looked to her left and found Marie to be in a bit of a world of her own. "You OK?"

"Huh? Yeah, I'm fine. I just started thinking about my husband, God rest his soul. He had his own business, and he killed himself working. What a guy."

"What kind of business was it?" the Greek lady asked.

"He had a hardware store. HARRY'S HARDWARE."

"HARRY'S HARDWARE??" Mable inquired with astonishment. "You don't mean in New Jersey, do you?"

"Yeah, Jersey. Petersville, near the port. Do you know it?"

"Know it? We used to live around the block from it growing up. My father used to go in there all the time."

"My God, this is unbelievable. Liz, did you hear that?"

By this time Elizabeth had awakened and did indeed hear the conversation.

"You know, a lot of people we know – they started out 'down the port,' as people would say. They say it like it was something bad. But I liked it. It was cozy and friendly and everyone knew each other. Best part of Elizabeth, if you ask me."

Marie was a bit taken aback since her sister usually didn't go on and on like that.

But she nodded in agreement, as did Mable, who continued where Liz left off...

"Yeah, that's where we lived when we first came to America. Most of our neighbors were Greek, though there were quite a few Italians and Polish as well. Yeah, that was a nice neighborhood all right. But then we moved after a few years. I guess my father wanted to be closer to where he worked, or maybe it was the school? I don't know."

"Mable, what did your father do?"

"He had a restaurant, what else would a Greek do? It was a small one, but they served great food. POP'S PLACE was the name."

"On Orchard Avenue, right?" Marie interjected. "My husband used to eat lunch there every day, and he would bring home what was left over. Your father served some big portions."

"At home, too," Mable said laughing, as she patted her belly.

The jovial trip down memory lane was suddenly interrupted by the captain's voice – "Ladies and gentlemen, we are about two hours from Los Angeles, and we've just been alerted about some turbulence a few minutes ahead. It's nothing to be concerned about, but just as a precaution, we'd like everyone to fasten their seat belts, as the signs indicate."

The warning "bell" and the seat belt sign were in synch with the captain.

"Shit, I knew we should have taken a goddamn train," Mable shouted, as she did a quick right face with her head directed at Marica, who tried to reassure her sister by staying calm and keeping her voice very matter-of-fact.

"He said it was nothing to be concerned about."

"If there's nothing to be concerned about why is everyone on the plane acting VERY concerned, huh?"

"Yeah, damned right!" Marie added, as she quickly blessed

herself – followed closely by her sister. Mable was already on her second go 'round with her fingers flying across her chest the requisite three times.

In the midst of all the turmoil and fear, Elizabeth had a question for their Cephalonian aisle mate.

"Mable, I've often wondered why Greeks bless themselves three times, and from right to left, rather than left to right, and only once, like Catholics do it."

Mable's face turned from panic to deliberation, as she looked up and thought and thought. The two Sicilians were waiting on the edge of their seats, literally, for her reply.

"Well, ladies, first of all, we say 'Cross' instead of 'Bless,' and we've been going right to left three times for close to two thousand years. Why do we do it that way? IT BEATS THE HELL OUT OF ME!!"

The three of them burst into gales of laughter, and even the solemn sister across the aisle cracked a smile. They never did hit any turbulence, at least in the air...

CHAPTER TEN

Meanwhile Back in Jersey

Mondays were rarely really good school days, and this was no exception. It was cold and what the weather channel would call "partly sunny," although the sun made the "partly" sound more like "barely." It was pretty much a typical March day in Jersey, but another downside if you had cafeteria duty was that none of the kids would eat their lunch outside, and it also cut down on the students opting to walk into town to grab a sandwich or coffee. So the lunch room was pretty much standing room only. It was also mid-marking period, which meant that if you were a teacher, all your grades had to be up to date, and if you were a student, there were deadlines that meant business. Maria had just been notified that she was to be observed on Tuesday, and it would be during what she called her "all or nothing" class because it seemed like they were either great or awful. Just what she needed – not knowing what to expect. After thirty years of teaching she had learned to roll the dice, and with the punches, but having her supervisor observe a more consistent class would have been nice. Plus she was behind on a few of the things she had to grade – and now this. She stormed into the cafeteria to find Nick among the missing. Where the hell was he? Of all the goddamn days to be out.

Nick wasn't "out" in the literal sense, though he was not "in" in the literal sense either. He had taken a half a personal day to drop his mother and aunt at the airport, and he was just entering the parking lot when he heard the bell sound, signaling the start of lunch. Shit. He hadn't told Maria he would be out in the morning because he figured he'd be back in plenty of time. Dumb. Of course, if he had her cell phone number, he could call her, but he didn't. Dumber. Now he would have to face what he assumed would be her death stare scowl. Dumbest. He screeched into a parking spot and made a run for the door, praying that what he had heard was the warning bell, and not the late bell. All the close spots had been taken, so he had to sprint a good sixty yards while listening for the second bell that would be at least a reprieve. It never came....because it had already sounded. He was a good ten minutes late when he burst upon the scene, mumbling every apology he could think of.

Maria had actually calmed down a bit by the time Nick came panting over to their table, but she figured she'd play the situation for all it was worth as she dialed up a face that would have frozen Mount Vesuvius.

"Sorry, Maria. I thought I'd make it back in time. I hadn't counted on the detours or Monday morning traffic." She was looking right at him, face to face, nose to nose, about six inches between them, and not a crease or an eyelash moved even a centimeter. She was biting her tongue to keep from bursting out with a rolling laugh, but she was a master of subterfuge, and Nick was literally petrified as the sweat started to run down the back of his neck, which was as tight as a drum.

The silence was finally broken by a tight-lipped, terse question that got right to the point "Where the hell were you??"

"Newark Airport."

"Newark Airport?"

"Yeah."

"Why didn't you just get on a plane while you were there? It would have been nice if you had told me on Friday. The principal's already been here twice wondering why *you* weren't here. I don't get paid to cover for you, nor to run this damn lunch by myself! Shape up, man!"

Maria had him exactly where she wanted. Just pick a metaphor, and that's where he was: *behind the eight ball; up shit's creek; strike two; not a leg to stand on...and on...and on....!*

To make matters worse, the principal walked in. It was in reality his first trip that day, but Nick thought it was his third, and he began a string of abject apologies that would have been confusing even if he had had his facts straight.

"Sorry, you missed me before, Mr. Morgan. I had to go to my car to get some manipulatives for this afternoon's classes, and also the software for my "Back To The Past" computer project for my history class.

This was all too much for the Sicilian. She had never heard Nick use the words "software" or "manipulatives" in his life – and with good reason, because he *had* never used them. She was laughing up such a storm inside that her eyes were tearing so much that even Morgan noticed.

"Are you OK, Maria?"

"Allergies," she managed to stutter.

The headman got a quizzical look on his face. It was too early for allergies, but he decided to let it slide since he was still trying to figure out what Nick meant by his apparently sincere apology. So, like all leaders from Caesar to the Queen, his reply was a statement that had nothing to do with anything.

"OK, then, catch you both later. Have a good day."

Maria could finally let her laughter go, and did it ever go, that is. Of course, she wasn't quite finished with Nick, so she used the principal as the pretense for her frivolity.

"Man, he can be a real idiot at times...."

Nick nodded in agreement.

"Just like you, you damn Greek. Now, would you be so kind as to explain what you were doing at Newark Airport on a Monday morning, and why you didn't tell me about it??"

Well, at least she was speaking to him now, so Nick figured he was slightly better off than he had been. He was still not out of the woods as the saying goes. In fact, he was pretty sure he didn't know the way out of the woods, so he figured he might as well stick with the truth, spoken in his subservient, apologetic, "mea culpa" tone, which he had become pretty good at.

"I was dropping my mother and my aunt off to catch their flight to California, and I meant to tell you Friday, but I was preoccupied with trying to catch up with my grades and I forgot all about it. Then this morning I figured I'd be back with plenty of time.to spare. Don't be mad, OK? Please?"

Maria cocked her head slightly and broke out into what appeared to be a smile, tiny as it was.

"Was that today they were leaving?"

As traumatized as he was, Nick just couldn't let a straight line like that go to waste.

"I sure as hell hope so. Otherwise, they're going to have to hitch a ride back!"

His partner's reply was a swat on the head with a stack of papers she had been reading.

"Guess who else is flying to California this morning, you dunderhead..."

Nick opened his mouth and was about to speak when she headed him off....

"And don't say 'lots of people'...you Greek clown!" Her tone had changed, and he could now see the clearing at the edge of the woods.

"Wait! Don't tell me your mom and aunt were going out this morning as well?"

"Uh, yeah. I told you last week they were leaving Monday! For a smart guy, you certainly do some dumb things."

Nick was about to say to her that there were a lot of "Mondays," but he thought he'd better leave it at that. She had told him, and he had totally forgotten all about it.

"Sorry, Maria. Yeah, you did tell me. Did you drive them out?"

"Nope. Cab. I couldn't take the drawn-out goodbyes I knew would happen if I drove them.."

Nick was surprised, and said so: "You sprung for a cab?"

"Hey, it was well worth it!"

Nick suddenly had an epiphany....

"You don't suppose they're on the same flight, do you? And that they somehow meet?"

"Hmm....I guess there's a possibility that they're on the same plane. But there must be a half dozen flights going out to the coast over the course of the morning, so chances are they're on a different one. But even if they're on the same plane, there have to be two hundred people on board, right ? What are the chances they'd run into each other? Believe me, if our mothers and aunts, respectively, meet up with each other, I'm pretty sure I'll hear about it." She didn't know it then, but Maria was foreshadowing some imminent earth-shaking events that were huge even for California.

CHAPTER ELEVEN

The City of Angels...??

The four Mediterranean Mothers were in different stages of consciousness as the plane ate up the miles across the country, passing over the Rockies and fast approaching California. Marica was looking out the window in between several cat-naps, while her sister had taken out some crocheting and was counting and looping and humming an old Greek song. Liz was out cold, but Marie was awake enough to watch Mable with a great deal of interest and admiration.

"Wow, that's really good. What are you making, if I may ask?"

"Just a shawl for my sister over there. She likes what I do, and it's my way of saying thanks to her. Even though I'm the older one she has done a lot for me, you know!"

Marie nodded her head.

"Yeah, we're like that, too. We always have each other's backs," Marie added as she pointed toward Liz, who was totally in the land of dreams.

Their sisterly admiration society was interrupted by the voice of the pilot indicating that they were about an hour away from the airport, and if anyone had anything to attend to this might be a good time to do it.

Marie decided to go for a final restroom visit, which gave Mable and Elizabeth the opportunity to talk a bit. Marica was resting ('sleeping'), so it was just the two of them for a few minutes.

Elizabeth looked over at her companion and smiled.

"You know, Mable, you're not fooling me with all that huff and gruff stuff. Know what I mean?"

"Not really, Liz, no." And she didn't. Well, sort of didn't.

Liz smiled and shook her head. "As my niece Maria would say: 'Please....' In fact, you remind me of her a little. She's tough as nails on the outside, but not on the inside – although, she doesn't want anyone to know it. Like you."

Mable was touched by what she felt was a compliment, which was how it was intended.

"Well, thank you. It's hard being the older one. You have to be tough, especially with my sister. Like I said, she's smart, but she still needs someone to look after her!"

Then she added with a chuckle – "Know what I mean?"

"I know exactly what you mean, Mable. Exactly."

For probably the first time in their lives, the two new friends high-fived, just as Marie was making her way back to her seat.

"So, talking about me, ladies?"

Mable couldn't resist.   "It's not always about you, Marie," which was really Liz's line, but what the heck!

The landing at LA Ex was smooth and uneventful, and the four of them approached it in the way most befitting each one's personality. Elizabeth and Marie worked their worry beads to a shiny luster, their eyes closed, of course, with prayers emanating from their faces like water over rapids. Marica calmly looked out the window, although she might have done a quick, almost imperceptible cross as the wheels touched down. Mable? Clutching the arm rest as if her life depended

73

on it, which to her seemed it did. Along the way she recited at record speed three "Our Fathers," two in Greek and one in English, and capped everything off, once the plane had come to a complete stop, with loud applause and a kiss for the aisle between the seats. The Sicilians pointed to her with respect, Marica shook her head, and the rest of the passengers gave her a standing ovation. Welcome to California!!

The ladies said their goodbyes to the crew of the plane, and whether it was because they provided somewhat of a diversion during the flight, or the personnel of the airline were glad to be rid of them – or a little bit of both – there were sincere smiles all around. The "Four Musketeers" had no problem finding the proper conveyor for their luggage, and they picked it up as easily as if they had been seasoned travelers. Of course, not to belittle native Californians, especially those who live in LA, their laid-back demeanor was no match for four tigers from New Jersey. They had their bags, a porter, and a taxi quicker than you could say Italians and Greeks. They were all a bit gassed from the trip, but they decided to meet the next day for dinner and talk about their first day and whatever else might come up. The taxi dropped the Mediterraneans at their respective hotels, but not before there had been hugs and kisses all around, even from the usually prim and proper Marica. So far, so good on this "Widows' Odyssey"!!

Their hotels were just a few miles from each other, and before they said their farewells, phone numbers, addresses, and seemingly enough information to complete a mortgage application changed hands several times. Everything got straightened out to everyone's satisfaction, and they were all looking forward to having a good time on Tuesday, their first full day in the City Of Angels. They promised to get in touch and make arrangements for dinner to rekindle their newly formed friendship and tell about their first day in California.

The four women were all pretty beat as they settled into

their hotel rooms. The Greeks were on the eighth floor and they had a great view of the city, which Mable absolutely loved as it reminded her both of her current apartment in New Jersey and her residence for forty years in Washington Heights, New York. Her sister took a peek out the window in between unpacking and putting her wardrobe in its proper place, which drew a comment from her older sister.

"A place for everything, and everything in its place, huh Marica?!"

"I just like to be organized. Aren't you going to unpack?"

"Maybe in a while. I want to call my daughter and tell her we got in all right. You want me to tell her to call Nick?"

"Might as well," Marica answered. "Nick's probably at work now, and he's never thrilled when I call him there. In fact, he's not thrilled when I call him anywhere." she said with a sigh. "Yeah, just ask Jo to call him later."

"Hey, he did give us this trip, right? That was nice," Mable responded as she fiddled with the phone in their room. A few misdials and several expletives later she was able to dial her daughter's number – only to get her voicemail. "Damn it all. Her stupid answering machine. Ugh! It was better in the old days with the old phone."

"Yeah, but at least now you can leave her a message," her sister reflected.

"I guess you're right"...."Hey, Jo, it's Ma. We got here OK. Give your cousin a call and let him know, and call me back when you get a chance. I left you all the Information on the hotel and everything. Love you. Ma."

She did love her daughter, and the feeling was mutual, although for a very long time the loads of guilt and mistrust had taken their toll. Jo Ann felt that her mother had been impossible to deal with and live with as she was growing up. Well, that's a story for another day, or at least another chapter, but suffice it to say that while most of the parents of Jo Ann's friends were somewhat controlling, Mable made a prison warden seem like a soft touch. She wouldn't let Jo Ann go to her prom, and Jo once told Nick that while she was growing up she hated her mother. Ah, but that was long ago, right...

The younger sister, serious as she usually was, did like to kid her older sibling when she got the chance, and this seemed like an easy one.

"You know, Melpo, you must be slipping as you're getting older. I'm just a bit disappointed in you!"

"What the hell you talking about??" To say this caught her off guard would be like a reverse hyperbole.

"Well, under normal circumstances, or perhaps when you were a bit younger, you would have gotten the skinny on just about everyone on that plane. Wha' happened?"

The usually stoic younger sister was loosening up. Actually, she would let her guard down once in a while, and maybe the trip to the coast was just what she needed.

"You know what happened as well as the next person. We ran into those two damn Sicilians and I couldn't shut that Marie up," Mable answered with a wide grin.

"She's probably saying the same thing about you right now."

Their analysis was interrupted by the phone.

"I got it," Mable volunteered. "Probably Jo Ann."

She grabbed the phone, assuming it was her daughter.

"Hey, just wanted to let you know we got here all right."

The answer was just a bit unexpected.

"I know you did, you damn Greek..We just dropped you off at your hotel. You getting senile on me, Melpomeni?"

"Marie?"

"Very good. I'm proud of you...."

"You think you're funny, huh?" Mable answered with a barrel-like laugh. "Well, you're not so funny!"

"We were just talking about you, you big-mouthed Greek."

"Yeah, same here, you frickin' Sicilian! What's up?"

"Well, Liz was just saying....why do we have to wait till tomorrow night to have dinner together? We got a lot of unfinished stories to tell."

"You're so right! I didn't even begin to tell you about all the heartaches my daughter dump on me!"

Marica had been listening in the background and, once more uncharacteristically, yelled out: "And I didn't even start!!"

Liz heard her across the rooms and across the miles.

"Was that the 'quiet one'?" she asked the older Greek. The two Sicilians thought that was a good moniker for Marica.

"Yup, it sure was," Mable answered. "I think being in California has done something to her – something good! Marica, the ladies want to know if we'd like to meet them for dinner tonight?"

"Hmm...that might be a good way to unwind, and then we can talk, and maybe I could get a word or two in. Yeah, let's go tonight!"

The question was what kind of food did everyone feel like, and how were they going to find a good restaurant?

CHAPTER TWELVE

Four for Dinner

Life can often be unpredictable, and it is hard to know what lies around the next bend, or in this case, in the next seat., Both sets of women had discussed the days happenings "intra-sister" and would later open up the conversation to include all four of the Mediterranean mothers. What were the odds that they would meet up with a somewhat mirror image of each other – albeit from across two seas – and also bond like gorilla glue. On the other hand, stepping back and examining the foursome, it seemed not only possible but inevitable that they would become the "Four" Musketeers, or perhaps the Fearsome Foursome, as Nick would later call them. They were, after all, widows, Mediterranean sisters, about the same ages, opinionated, and hell-bent on exacting many pounds of flesh from their progeny via years and years of intense and continuous histrionics and guilt trips, tears and smiles, scoldings and love. What a recipe for raising kids! Just standard fare for those of Italian or Greek descent.

So now that they decided *when* to eat, the question became *where* to eat! The two more talkative of the foursome were on the phone discussing that very thing as Marica and Liz offered their input to their sisters from across their respective hotel rooms.

"Hey, Marie, I don't care where we go as long as they have some Ouzo or Metaxa," Mable began with a smile that could probably be seen over the phone.

"So, you overbearing Greek," Marie replied kiddingly. "We meet you today and right away you want to take charge. I should have known. Actually, though, Greek food doesn't sound too bad. And something to wash it down besides coffee. Hmm. That might work."

Marica could sense the gist of the conversation, and interjected her opinion quickly and vociferously.

"That's OK with me, but it's got to be a *good* place, not some hole in the wall."

"Marie, my snooty sister wants to be sure it's a *good* place, not some hole in the wall and I quote her exactly."

Marie was transcribing her conversation for her sister, although Liz pretty much could tell what was happening, and the two Sicilians and Mable went into a belly laugh contortions. Even Marica cracked a smile.

"OK, smart ass," Mable said to her sister. "How do we find a good place?"

"Well, we could ask them at the front desk. They should know about restaurants and what they serve. And the reputations they have among the people. After all, the hotel workers live here."

"Did you hear that, Marie? My sister wants to ask the people at the front desk."

"Well, that might work, but..."

Her thoughts were interrupted by a quick question from Elizabeth.

"What might work?"

"Asking them at the desk."

Liz shook her head. "Don't like that idea. How do we know

we can trust the desk clerks? Maybe they have a relative who owns a place, or maybe they're getting paid off to send their guests somewhere. We need to talk to someone we can trust!"

Then the proverbial light bulb went off over Marie's head! "Let's call Maria!"

CHAPTER THIRTEEN

When the Cat's Away…

It was about five o'clock on the west coast – around eight back in the East. It was also "College Night" where Maira and Nick teach, and they were both involved with various presentations. They lived within a few blocks of each other, so they decided to come in together, and since Maria's meetings were right across the hall from Nick's room, she dumped her purse and things on his desk.Maria's talk had already started when her phone went off, catching Nick not only off guard but also with very few options. He usually didn't answer other people's cells, but of course he knew her mom was out in California, and he was afraid it might be an emergency, either real or imagined. So he discreetly crossed himself and picked up the call.

"Hello, Maria? It's your mother. I'm calling from California."

The next four words would live on as a turning point in his sanity.

"Hi. This is Nick."

"*WHO* Is this?"

"Nick. Nick Pappas."

"Who the hell are you?"

"I teach with Maria. Maybe she told you about me."

"Why do you have her phone? Is she all right?"

"She's fine. She's right across the hall."

"Across the hall? Across the hall? Are you at her house?"

Nick started to chuckle, which was definitely the wrong thing to do.

"No, no. We're at school. We're at college night. See…"

Before he could finish Marie had a memory flashback and literally jumped through the phone as she exploded:

"Now I remember that name. Pappas. You're the damn Greek who has lunch duty with her, right?"

Once again Nick's choice of words left much to be desired: "guilty as charged."

"I'll bet!!!" Marie stated emphatically.

Meanwhile, Liz, Mable, and yes, even Marica, wondered what was happening, and to complicate things just a bit back in the East, Maria had left her speaker on and half the parents In Nick's session, who were waiting for things to start, wore puzzled looks as they tried to figure out the context of this surprising conversation. Of course, this was nothing new for Nick. He was used to taking a touchy situation and making it into an explosive one, and he lived up to this track record once more.

When the parents looked up at him for some sort of explanation about the "slightly emotional" female voice on the phone, there were a number of things he could have done to mitigate the damage and several things to make things worse. Of course, he chose something from the second group as he addressed the curious multitude.

"Hi, welcome to college night. My name is Nick Pappas, history, and I suppose you're all wondering about the person on the phone. Not a big deal, really, just a little mixup. She's just trying to talk with her daughter, who left her phone in here, and she sort of doesn't trust people…well men….who work with her. Men who work with her daughter, not her. Well, I mean she tends to be suspicious, and she is calling from three thousand miles away."

Nick was sweating profusely, and he was speaking faster and faster, a sure sign of panic. As he looked over those assembled, he almost felt he was in the middle of a class judging by the wide range of looks in people's eyes, which went from disbelief to laughter, and every stop in between.

Like a relief pitcher from the bullpen, Maria walked in to try to save the day. Luckily her group was on a break because there was no telling where things in Nick's room were headed. Maria had heard just enough to realize what was happening. She grabbed the phone, gave Nick a look and a wink, and apologized to the assembled parents and ducked into the hallway, turning off the speaker as she went.

"OK, Mom. What's going on?"

"What's going on? What's going on? Don't you think I should be asking *you* what's going on? I call to find out about a restaurant and I find myself in the middle of a modern *PEYTON PLACE....*"

Maria knew how her mother's mind worked, and though she was usually ready for just about anything, this caught her off guard just a bit.

"PEYTON PLACE?"

"Yeah, Maria, you know, the movie about the town where everyone is fooling around with everybody else!"

"I know the reference. What does that have to do with tonight?"

"Please, Maria. All I tried to do was get in touch with my daughter, and I get this damn Greek on the phone instead, and he's in some sort of 'meeting,' he says. I can just picture what's going on. Why does he have your phone, and where are you?"

Maria was in a precarious position because there were people constantly walking by, so she had to keep both her emotions and her voice low, but she couldn't stop herself from shaking her head and displaying the wry grin of all time as she rolled her eyes and almost shook her head out of its socket. This was like talking with Nick...

"First of all, how are things going on the coast? Are you and Liz OK?"

"Never mind changing the subject. Yeah, we're good *here*. How are things *there*? Or shouldn't I ask, 'Why does this Greek have your phone?' What's all that noise that I hear. Some kind of party? When the cat's away, Maria. When the cat's away."

"WHAT??"

"Very convenient. Your husband's on a business trip to Italy, and you send us packing to California. Quite a coincidence that we're all gone at the same time. Is there something you're not telling me?"

"Ma, listen....we had a meeting at school and we had to bring in a lot of stuff, so we just came in together. He lives about a half mile from me, that's all, so he picked me up."

"And then he's going to drop you off at your house? Listen, Maria, I didn't just get off the boat!"

The parents were changing rooms to go to different presentations, and the hall was filling up quickly, so Maria needed to end this as soon as possible.

"Ma, I'll talk to you about this tomorrow, OK? I really gotta go. Was there something you wanted?"

"You'd better believe we'll talk about it young lady or you're going to have to live with this guilt your whole life. How could you do this to your mother?"

Marie hung up and never did ask Maria about the restaurant. The next session was just about to start, and Nick quickly poked his head into the hall and caught Maria as she was stepping into her assigned room.

"Not good, huh Maria?"

She shook her head.

"Tell you about it on the way home, just don't get fresh you damn Greek," she said out of the corner of her mouth with just a hint of a smile.

"Huh" Nick exclaimed, for probably the five millionth time in his life.

"This is enough to make a girl start drinking....tonight." Maria thought to herself as she walked into her classroom. The parents were already there.

"Hi! I'm Maria Orlando. Let's see about getting your kids into college!"

CHAPTER FOURTEEN

Where Italians and Greeks Come to Eat

Marie told her sister about her conversation with her daughter complete with suspicions and threats – all directed at Nick. She vowed to get to the bottom of things once they got home at the very latest, but she was, after all not only Sicilian, but a widowed mother. What a combination! Had Nick known the tenuous position he was in there's not telling what he would have done. Although, the truth of the matter was that there was rarely a time that one could predict what Nick would do. Not even Nick!

While Marie was debating the fate that awaited the unsuspecting Greek in Jersey the hotel phone buzzed. It was Mable.

"Guess what, Marie! My daughter called!"

"Yeah, well, guess what, Mable. I called *MY* daughter! Wait till you hear what's going on with this guy she works with!"

"Can you tell us at dinner? Jo Ann said there's a really good place that serves Greek *and* Italian. It's called 'Where *ITAL-IANS AND GREEKS – Come To Eat'* She said it's usually called just *ITALIANS AND GREEKS!* Supposed to have a good variety of food to pick from. Even my sister says it seems all right. How about you two? Sounds like a pretty good name!"

Marie and Liz held a quick caucus and it was unanimous.

"We're all good here, Mable. Do you want us to meet you at your hotel, or do you want to come here?"

Mable was hungry, and it didn't make any difference as long as they got going fairly soon.

"I'll have my sister call and make reservations for six thirty, and we'll grab a cab and pick you up in about an hour or so. How about that?"

"You got it, 'Melpomeni.'"

"Hey, Marie, that was really good. I'll make a Greek out of you yet," Mable answered with a laugh.

"Heaven forbid, Mable, heaven forbid," Marie grinned. "See you soon."

Before you could say "guilt trip" the four ladies were seated comfortably in a taxi headed for dinner. Marica was her usual prim self as she settled into her seat, Liz was commenting on all the sights of LA, Mable's stomach was growling, and Marie was so happy with the transportation that she temporarily put aside her recent run-in with Nick and Maria. She turned to her Greek compatriot.

"Mable, where did you find this cab? It's so comfortable and it has so much room to stretch out!"

"I can't take the credit. My sister did everything. She got it."

"Thank you, Marica!" Marie proclaimed. "Thank you. Hey, is it OK if I call you 'Rica'"? Marica, for her part, just nodded and smiled. It was the first time Marie had addressed Marica directly, but it wouldn't be the last!

"I love to stretch out while we're driving. There is so much room. You should see my nephew's car. You can barely turn your head," Mable proclaimed, exaggerating just a bit. Her observation drew a laugh from her sister and a comment from Marie.

"Yeah, just like Maria's car. Right, Liz? I think it was made for midgets." Her comment drew giggles all around, including the driver, but it also reminded Marie about her recent altercation with Nick and her daughter. She was about to "tell all" "to all," but the cab was just pulling up in front of their destination, so the story of intrigue and deception would have to wait – but only for a bit!

CHAPTER FIFTEEN

Friends Old and New

Before you could say "I'm starving," the cab pulled up to a very homey looking restaurant perched on the corner of two very picturesque streets. "ITALIANS & GREEKS" was highlighted in large, soft neon lights, with *Where....Come To Eat.* completing the name. The lights were a pleasing combination of light blue, purple, and crimson, and the restaurant had a traditional, inviting brick front which complimented the lighting and welcoming feeling it exuded.

A courteous doorman let them in and greeted them in Italian, Greek, and English, which pleased the guests more than one could imagine, and before you know it the ladies were seated at a very nice table with a beautiful view of the city. No fuss, no problems. Of course, they couldn't leave well enough alone; there had to be a comment, or rather a complaint, tied to their offspring.

Marie led off.

"Hey Liz, remember the last time we went out to eat? About a month ago. We were at my house and Maria took us out to the diner?"

For her part, Liz was already scanning the menu and had to ask her sister to repeat what she had said.

"That diner, Liz, where we went with Maria. Remember?"

"Oh yeah, the diner, couple weeks ago. Yeah. They had good food there."

"Well, they did. But do you remember how long it took us to find a table? I thought it was the damn Greek who ran the place, but now I'm thinking it was Maria This place is probably run by Greeks and it was smooth as anything getting seated.!" Marie emphasized her revelation with a snap of a breadstick.

"Hmmm, You might be right, Marie. I mean, Maria tries to help but I think sometimes it would be simpler without her," Liz answered.

Mable, meanwhile, had been nodding her head vigorously.

"I know just what you mean. When Jo Ann goes out with me she tries to take charge, like I was some kind of helpless old lady. Drives me crazy. And what's even worse is when her god damn idiot of a husband comes with us. I feel like killing him."

"Yeah, ladies, well, at least your kids *take* you out. My son hasn't done that since....lord, I can't even remember when the last time was When he was growing up we used to take him out to eat with us all the time, and then after his father died I would take him out every chance I had. You'd think he would remember that and return the favor. Nope. He acts as if I had some kind of disease, or that he's just embarrassed to be seen with me. I mean, it's the least he could do, don't you think ladies?"

"Damn right, Marica!" Marie exclaimed. "I know just how you feel."

Mable and Liz nodded vigorously.

"Don't expect nothing, Ricky, cause you're not gonna get nothing," Mable lectured her sister. "I tell you a hundred times."

Their complaints were interrupted by a smiling waitress, who brought a tray of bread, olives, and cheese for pre-dinner snacking, along with a "side order" of oregano, olive oil, pepper....the works. Mable, never shy, grabbed a piece of feta and a slice of Italian bread to get herself started. This drew a disdainful look from her sister, but the older Greek didn't care.

"You could have waited till she left, Mable."

"Hey, she brought it for us to eat, and I'm hungry. Anyway, I think better on a full stomach."

"Think? What do you have to think about?"

"I gotta think what I want for dinner. Ti kopsimo se troey?"

Mable's forceful rebuttable elicited laughter from the Sicilian sisters, even though they weren't quite sure about the meaning of the last four words.

The server, who was laughing herself, decided to help with the translation.

"It's an old Greek saying, and it means 'what's it to you?' But the literal translation would be 'what cramp is gnawing at you?'"

This brought more laughter all around, even from the usually prim and proper Marica, who thanked the lady for her help and complimented her on the explanation.

"I apologize, ladies, for not introducing myself. I got caught up in your conversation. My name is Christina, and it will be my pleasure to serve you tonight. This looks like a fun group. You guys must be good friends, huh?"

Marie jumped in with a big grin...

"Yeah, I guess we are good friends, huh, Mable?"

"You bet we are. Greeks (as she pointed to herself and her sister) and Sicilians (waving at Marie and Liz). The best of friends." Even Marica had to smile.

"Well, that's me, Greek and Sicilian. My father's Greek, my mom's Sicilian!"

This was too much...!!

All of the women were a bit taken aback by this revelation. Coincidence is coincidence, but this seemed like it might be something more.

Liz was the first to voice her surprise, and her comment was short and to the point: "Wow!"

"You got that right. You got that right!" Mable shot in. She rarely repeated anything so vociferously, and when she did it served as a double exclamation! "Something is going on here!"

Marie threw in a "Holy Cow," and even Marica chirped in with a "Hmmm," and nodded with an expression on her face that her sister always called "The Look."

Christina smiled but seemed just a bit puzzled at the reaction to her ethnic background. Marie decided to explain things and turned her head toward the slightly confused waitress.

"You were right when you said we appeared to be 'good friends,' cause I think we are, right ladies?" (There were nods all around). "But the truth of the matter is that we just met these Greek ladies on the plane coming out here today. They were sitting next to us, and we got to talking...." She passed the baton to Mable, who was more than happy to continue with the story of this apparent Odyssey   .

"...and it turns out we have so many things in common. We're all from New Jersey, two sets of widows..."

"....with ungrateful, disobedient kids," Marie added.

"And we're all from islands near Italy and Greece," Marica surprisingly contributed to the geography lesson.

"You know we're Sicilians," Liz reiterated.

"And we were born in Cephalonia," Mable stated proudly.

Christina's jaw dropped to her chest, and she broke out with a coast to coast smile. "Cephalonia?? That's where my father and his brothers were born. This is unbelievable!"

"You got that right, kid! You got that right." The four of them more or less shouted.

"My dad is off tonight, but my mother is here. She's back in the kitchen. I'm sure she'd like to meet you, but she's talking a new cook through the steps of a new dish, so she's a bit tied up right now. Wait till I tell her!!"

In all the excitement Christina turned and started to walk away without getting a single order. She was back in a flash with an embarrassed look on her face that was buried in her smile and apology.

"I'm so sorry ladies. I didn't take your orders."

"No apology needed," Marie sincerely replied.

Christina appeared relieved, but she was still smiling incredulously, as were the ladies.

"May I make a suggestion? My parents created a dish which is a combination of Greek and Sicilian cuisine. It's got a little bit of everything, and they named it 'Heaven On A Plate.' Would you like to try it?"

There were nods all around.

"Great!" Christina smiled. "I'll be right back with the salads to start you off!"

"See how easy it is without the kids here!" Marie proclaimed.

CHAPTER SIXTEEN

College Night Winding Down...

Despite all the extra-curricular problems courtesy of the West Coast, the night actually went pretty well, as parents came and went and Nick got his feet back under him. Of course, there had to be a wrinkle in the works, and it soon showed its face in the person of Brad Morgan, the principal. He was going from class to class and making his presence known, which was actually what he was supposed to be doing as the head guy. It put sort of an official stamp on the event, and it was good PR for the school as he said hello to different groups of parents at the various sites. And then he stuck his shiny bald head into Nick's room. One group of parents had just left and there was to be one more meeting in about ten minutes. The principal was not a welcome sight, although it did add a bit of levity to the night as the fluorescent lights danced and twinkled off of the top of Morgan's head. Nick scrunched his mouth into a knot to keep from chuckling out loud.

"Mr. Pappas, how's it going?" he asked with a phony smile.

"Not bad, not bad at all," was the reply from Nick. He figured that was about as non-committal as he could get. In fact, he said it a third time for extra emphasis but mostly to piss off the principal, who hated when things were repeated.

"Yes, Nick, I heard you the first thirty times," was Morgan's sarcastic response.

"Good hyperbole, Brad. Very nice," Pappas responded.

"It was actually an understatement...."

Nick decided to put an end to the tennis match of insults back and forth. He knew he could "one up" the principal indefinitely, but he wanted to get him out as soon as possible before the last group came in. Then he could get them out a bit quicker. Sort of a domino effect!

"I actually have one more presentation in a few minutes. Was there something else?" Nick tried to be as diplomatic as possible, which was normally a chore for him even talking with someone he liked, much less this dolt.

"Well, yes, there was. I understand you took a phone call during one of your sessions? You know that's a 'no-no,' right?"

Damn. One of the parents had ratted him out. Nick pinched the back of his thigh as hard as he could to keep himself from cursing out the unknown stoolie and to stop himself from pointing out that Brad had just repeated the 'no' sound three times. The "high road" was foreign to Nick, but he navigated it pretty well.

"Yes, I am aware of that protocol. But it was a family emergency. Thanks for understanding."

Morgan was ready for a confrontational statement, and like a batter getting a change up when he was expecting a fastball, this caught him totally by surprise.

"Well, this...uh, sure. Things happen," he stammered as he turned and walked out into the hall. "Have a good night."

Nick released the smile he had been holding in, and it was perfect timing as the final troop of mothers and fathers sauntered in.

CHAPTER SEVENTEEN

The Long Ride Home...

By the time the principal gave his "thanks for coming and have a good evening" speech over the intercom it was pushing ten o'clock. Why he had to say anything, and why any of the parents stayed to hear it was beyond comprehension, but, as people say, "it is what it is," and what it was, was, very late on a school night, with still more than half the week to go. Nick grabbed his car keys, Maria grabbed her purse, and they were off to the car, their path lined with the epithets cascading out of their mouths like mouthwash at a dentist's office.

"Why don't they start these damn nights earlier, or at least do them on a Thursday night, so we'd have only one day to go? Do you realize the week is just beginning?" It was Maria at her fire-eyed best.

All Nick could do was nod in agreement. Anything he said would be gilding the lily, as the saying goes. He was pretty good at complaining, but when it came to sheer vitriol, no one could top Maria. Or even come close.

As they were getting into the car he said something he knew he should not have, but after thousands of times doing just that, what difference would one more make?

"Maria, I know I probably shouldn't ask you this, but is everything OK with your Mom?"

She turned and gave him the death stare, and she didn't have to verbalize what she was thinking: "If you know you shouldn't be asking, then why the hell are you??"

He answered her unspoken query out loud...

"Yeah, yeah...I know...."

It was a scenic drive between the high school and the town in which they lived; the winding roads through the hills and past literally hundreds of trees made coming to work – and going home – a pleasant experience. Well, at least most of the time. By now it was well past ten and the scarcity of lights, which heightened the country feel in the daytime, made the night drive a bit hazardous. It wasn't made any easier by Maria's continual harangue at the phone for having poor reception and at Nick for "barely missing" several large trees. In reality, he hadn't come that close to them, but he knew that something unpleasant or embarrassing would come from the transcontinental communication between mother and daughter, so for once he kept quiet.

"I may as well wait till we get to my house. I need a minute or two to gather my thoughts." She glanced at the dashboard...."Hey Greek, you're going ten miles under the speed limit. Let's go, huh?"

There is a limit to anyone's resolve to go against their first instinct, and this constant nitpicking was more than Nick could tolerate even without an impending crisis at hand. Luckily, his comment was direct and non-provocative without any of his usual sarcastic inflection.

"Sorry, I thought you said you needed a moment or two."

His companion was about to give him what for when they turned the corner of her street. Nick was actually a bit astonished because it looked like Maria was somewhat apprehensive about the forthcoming call. He had rarely seen that expression on her face, so he decided to put away his "humorous" persona for the rest of the evening.

"You wanna just leave all the school stuff in my car?" he asked, as he pulled into her driveway.

"Yeah, either in your car or go back and dump it in the river!"

Ah, there was the woman he knew and loved.

"Hey, Nick, could you do me a favor?"

"Sure!"

"Stay here while I make the call. Just for moral support"

Nick had to use all his powers to clam up with a straight line like that. Given her mother's accusations from earlier in the evening, he was dying to make "moral" into "immoral," and then perhaps add a comment of his own. But, for the second time within the space of about an hour, Nick Pappas was a better man and took that little-travelled high road.

"Whatever you need me to do, you got it." Was knowing Maria actually making him a better human being? First with the principal, and now with this panicky Sicilian. He shook his head and dismissed that thought out of hand. No way. Or, as Maria might have said had she been privy to his mental battle with himself – "PLEASE..."

CHAPTER EIGHTEEN

We Don't Really Drink

While Maria and Nick were playing a guessing game as to the happenings in California, the four widows were off to a rip-roaring start to their evening. Christina not only brought the salads, which looked mouth-watering and turned out to be delicious, but also a double round of drinks – Disaronno and Metaxa for each of their guests.

"Oh, I don't think we ordered these," Marica began as the glasses were deftly placed in front of the ladies."

"And we don't really drink," Marie added.

"Speak for yourself, you damn Italian," Mable chided her while taking a big gulp of the Greek brandy. "Speak for yourself."

"Oh, everyone who dines with us gets something complimentary to sip on before dinner," Christina explained. "But when I told my mother about who you were and where you were from – she said to double the drinks and keep them coming!"

"That works for me," Liz added.

"Me, too," said the suddenly loquacious Marica, as she downed one and was halfway through the second.

"What the heck, I don't wanna break up the party," Marie concluded with a flourish of clinking glasses with her sister and friends and two big gulps of delicious booze!"

Their unbridled revelry was almost interrupted by a three-thousand-mile phone call, courtesy of Maria, who hit her mother's name on her phone, but after a few rings, it went right to voicemail. She tried again with the same result. Apparently not only drinking and driving don't mix, drinking and hearing a cell phone don't either. An apprehensive look spread across Maria's face as she turned toward Nick.

"Something's wrong, Nick. Something's wrong. My mother always has her phone with her, especially when she's somewhere other than her house. Why doesn't she answer?"

Nick was rarely any good in a crisis, but for once he appeared to have things under control, his mouth included.

"Hey, she probably is in the bathroom or maybe she stepped out onto her balcony. It's around eight out there, right? Maybe she's having a late supper. Just give it another shot."

These were unfamiliar waters for Nick. Usually, he went off half-cocked (no pun intended) and Maria was calm and cool. It actually gave him a good feeling – not to see her upset – but for once to play the rock instead of a flighty feather at the mercy of every slight gust of emotion.

"OK, I'll give it another shot. Thanks, Nick," Maria said sincerely as she squeezed his hand, took a deep breath, and pushed the button on her phone.

"Hello!" Maria's eyes lit up!

"Thank goodness, she got her," Nick surmised.

"Hi, Mom?"

"Yeah! Jo Ann? How did you get this number?," replied the voice from California.

"Jo Ann? This is Maria. Who is this?"

"This is Mable. Who is this?"

"Maria! Where is my mother? And who are you??"

"I'm Mable. Oh, wait. Wait a minute...." Came the response, as the lady on the west coast put down the phone.

Maria turned to Nick with her logic in disarray.

"Nick, someone has my mother's phone. Someone named Mable!"

Nick's eyes almost popped through the windshield.

"Mable? Mable??"

Meanwhile, the aforementioned Mable had given the phone to Marie, laughing all the while.

"Sorry, I picked up your phone by mistake. I thought it might be for me."

This was too much for Marica.

"Mable, how the heck could that be for you? Neither of us has a cell phone!"

Marica was not in the habit of cracking jokes, and this was about as far from a funny line as you could get. Yet it sent the four of them into howls of laughter. This was not lost on Maria, who was getting more bewildered by the second.

"Mom, is that you? It's Maria! Is everything all right?"

"Yup, it's your mother. Is this my daughter?"

"Ma, I just told you it's Maria...:"

"Well, there are thousands of Marias in this country. How do I know it's you and not some other Maria? Answer me that if you can!"

"Mother, have you been drinking?"

Marie pulled away from the phone and addressed the other three women:

"Someone named Maria wants to know if we've been drinking! What about it ladies....have we? Let's take a vote... Maria my daughter or just plain Maria, my sister Liz and our two Greek lady friends unanimously feel that you're damn right we've been drinking"

This sent them into an encore of their guffaws, only they

were louder and longer.

"Ma, look. I'll call you in the morning, OK?"

"OK by me. And remember, whoever you are, and whatever you've done, you can always go to confession!"

Maria shook her head in desperation and clicked the phone off to another chorus of laughs. She turned to Nick in disbelief.

"My mother never drinks, but she just vehemently stated that she and my aunt and two Greek women were all getting plowed. AND....she said I should go to confession! Nick, did you hear me? Confession!"

This was within a whisper of Nick's self-control, which was not that great to begin with. THREE TIMES in one night. Yes, three times, and somehow he had kept himself calm and even rational. And to top it off, the last two were with Maria. CONFESSION? Give me strength, he said over and over. Maybe it was divine intervention, or maybe he was just due for a stable response – but whatever it was, he managed to keep both his libido bottled up and his mouth shut, as he shifted gears.

"Yeah, I heard you. I heard you. But listen, the first woman you talked to...her name was Mable?"

"Yeah, so?"

"So, that's my aunt's name!"

"Holy crap, Nick. Holy crap."

"You can say that again, Maria!"

"Holy crap, Nick, you're in the wrong driveway."

CHAPTER NINETEEN

Stories and More Stories

Back on the "Left Coast," as Easterners often say, things were rolling right along, and the musketeers were traveling all over the map of their minds and their memories.

"What shall we drink to," Marica asked, as she downed another gulp of Disaronno. "You know, this drink is pretty good, and I never drink. Do I Mable?"

"You're full of shit you never drink my little sister. You never let anyone *see* you drink."

"Well, isn't that the same thing? Isn't it? Well, isn't it?" Marica paused to let the other ladies ponder her question, and to allow Christina to serve their specialty dish.

"Wow, this looks delicious," Marie proclaimed, as she took a big whiff of the steaming hot main course. "And, no, Marica, I don't think it's quite the same thing."

"Yeah, it's like the tree falling in the forest. I think it makes a sound whether or not someone is there to hear it!" Elizabeth piggybacked.

The only other sounds emanating from the mouths of the "babes" over the next few minutes were a few "Hmmms" but mostly "Ummms" as they tasted and then began to heartily devour the fare in front of them.

The food and the liquor and the company soon turned the evening into stories about who they were and why they had hit it off so famously and so quickly.

"You know," Marie said thoughtfully between forkfuls of spinach pie and bites of both feta and provolone, "I think you two ladies are really interesting. I mean, you could do a feminine Abbott and Costello skit very easily. You're very different, and yet you're a great team!"

"Maybe it's *because* we're so different!" Mable proclaimed.

"She's right there." Marica agreed wholeheartedly. "My sister is outgoing and talkative and very mischievous."

"Yeah, and *my* sister is prim and proper and smart as all get outs!"

"We figured that out pretty quickly," Liz added. "Pretty quickly!"

"You think you've seen the real Mable? You ain't seen nothing! Let me tell you a couple stories about my big sister. May I?"

"By all means," the Sicilians said almost in unison. "By all means."

"OK, girls, you asked for it," Marica warned. "Grab a drink and hold on while I take you back a few years."

"Thelo na pau mazi sou," said the little girl. She was about four and a half, and full of the devil.

"Oxi!" said her mother rather emphatically.

Her mother and father, Nick's grandparents, usually went out to work in the fields. Sometimes they would take Mable with them, sometimes they didn't. This day happened to be one that she would be left at home. That usually meant there was an extra amount to do and it would be easy to lose track of their little girl. She would be safer at the house, and her mom's cousin would probably stop by to check on her. Made sense, but not to Mable, who felt that she had asked very nicely, and that her mother's one-word answer – "No!" – was not acceptable. So she just put on a downcast mask and whimpered softly.

"You play. We will be back before you know it," her mother said half consolingly.

However, "play" was not in Mable's plans for this day. The operative word was revenge. Her mother had about a dozen beautiful plants in pots displayed rather decoratively around the patio adjoining their modest house. There was a wide variety of blossoms, everything from roses to violets, and they were her pride and joy. Though it took the better part of the morning and a lot of sweat and exertion, the little girl managed to separate each of them from its respective receptacle and place it neatly on the ground. "That will show her," Mable thought to herself. "They're not going to leave me home again." And they didn't. Of course, she wasn't able to sit down for a few days, but it was worth it, as she thought of a particular plant with each swat her father administered.

The Sicilians looked at her in awe.

"Weren't you afraid of what your parents would do to you?" It was Marie who asked what seemed to be the obvious question.

"Nah, not really. I just wanted to get even with them for leaving me home. And I did!"

Liz took a different tack: "Didn't you feel guilty about what you did to your mother's plants?"

"Why should I? They sure as heck didn't feel guilty about leaving me home all by myself! They started it by leaving me all alone!"

As the ladies were getting the scoop from the plant perpetrator, Christina stopped back to see if everything was OK and whether the ladies needed anything else at the moment.

"Maybe another round?" Marica asked as she downed her remaining brandy.

"And, Christina," Liz joined in. "This dish you recommended is the best thing I've ever had!"

"Yes," Marie quickly added. "It is heavenly indeed!"

"Well, I'm delighted you like my dish," said a voice from a sultry-looking fiftyish lady coming up behind the waitress. "I'm Gina, Christina's mother" She made a hand gesture to her daughter to get another round, and one for her as well. "My husband, Ted and I run this establishment, and the 'piece of heaven' was sort of my idea."

"Bravo! Bravo!" Mable proclaimed   as she clapped her hands, a gesture in which she was soon joined by the other diners.

Marie did the introductions, including nationalities, as Gina exchanged handshakes and hugs with the fearsome foursome.

"I understand you just met, and yet you're good friends, right?" Gina tasted. They all nodded. "It's obvious how well you get along and fit together. Must be the Mediterranean in you. Would you mind if I joined you for a bit?"

"Would we mind?" Mable began....

"...we weren't gonna let you go!" Marie completed the thought.

"Please, sit down," Liz continued. "Rica was just telling us some stories from the time her sister was a little girl in Cephalonia."

"Ah, Cephalonia! My husband talks about it all the time. He was from a small village called Cardia. It means 'heart.'"

The Greeks suddenly became transfixed with their mouths open a country mile.

The three Sicilians' expressions all asked the same thing: "what's the matter?"

"That's the village we were born in," the Greeks said almost in unicorn.

As if it were choreographed, Christina had just returned with the brandy.

"A toast to Cephalonians, Sicilians, and my new friends," shouted Gina with a flourish. They all took a big sip and smiled. What an evening this was turning out to be.

"I believe someone said something about a story from the old country?"

"You're up again, Rica," Liz remarked.

"OK. I think you'll like this one even more...So you have to remember my sister was about five, and she was already on the road to being the biggest kidder and con artist you'd ever want to meet. Now, our village was up in the mountains, and while it was not very large, the houses were spread out a bit from each other, and the paths were very uneven and stony. One day Mable met a friend of hers walking toward the edge of the village. The little boy was carrying a rather large dish covered with a very elegant red dinner napkin, and he was walking very slowly and watching every step.

Besides being mischievous, Mable was always curious about everything, and this rather unusual situation piqued her interest.

"Hi, Ted, where are you going?"

"To my Yiayai's house."

"Why are you going there?"

"Well, she's not feeling well, so my mother made her some food and I'm taking it to her."

Mable shook her head, explaining to the lad that his grandmother lived such a long way off and that he didn't have to walk all the way over there. She could be very convincing.

"I don't?" questioned her patsy. "What do you mean?"

"That is a magic plate. All you have to do is let go of it, and it will get to your Yiayia's on its own."

"Wow! I didn't know that. Are you sure?"

"Swear to God," said the flim-flam artist extraordinaire.

So the boy let go of the plate and it smashed to pieces on the rocks beneath their feet. Ted went home crying, and Mable went home to another spanking. But she was laughing all the way.

Of course, all four of the musketeers were laughing, including Marica the storyteller and Mable the "star."

"Come on, Mable. Did this really happen?" Marie wondered.

"Oh, it happened all right. It happened!" It was Gina. "And I've heard that story many times….many times…"….she continued with a smile as wide as the Ionian Sea…."many times!"

"*You've heard it?*" Marica asked in amazement.

"You've heard it?" Marie echoed.

"From who, Gina?" Liz interjected

"Yeah, from who," asked Mable, the most puzzled of all.

The crowd at the restaurant was starting to thin out, so Christina had stayed for "story hour."

"I've heard it too, at just about every family gathering. Should I tell them Ma?"

Gina nodded vigorously.

"I heard it a thousand times, it seems like – and each time it gets funnier."

The guests were on the edge of their seats….

"I HEARD IT FROM MY FATHER! He's the one you got (pointing to Mable) to drop the plate. Wait till we tell him."

Gina, meantime, was on her phone.

"Hey Ted, you need to come down here right away. Yeah, I know it's your night off and a special on the Dodgers is coming on….And no, I can't tell you why. Just get your Greek ass down here."

She looked around the table and winked!

CHAPTER TWENTY

It's Been a Long Time

"Mable!" was the first thing Ted Micropolis said as he walked toward the table in his restaurant. "It's been a few years, huh? *Ti Kanis?*"

Gina was stunned, as was everyone else.

"Christina, did you tell your father what this was all about?"

"Not a word, Mom, honest," said the equally flabbergasted waitress, shaking her head. The other ladies were just as thunderstruck by what appeared yet another outlandish coincidence. The six of them looked at the owner, who smiled broadly and explained.

"It's very simple, really. The last time I saw a look like that on anyone's face was about fifty-some-odd years ago on a small path in Cardia. That sly, foxlike countenance becomes you, Melpo. Welcome to *ITALIANS AND GREEKS!*"

There were smiles and hugs all around, even before introductions, which were carried out with another round of drinks served by Ted himself.

"Before you ask, dear, these are all widows from New Jersey – two sets of sisters who apparently became good friends in less than a day," Gina explained.

Her daughter did the ethnic background – "Two Sicilians (pointing to Marie and Liz), and, as you must have deduced, two Cephalonians. They all met on the plane coming out this afternoon. Pretty cool, huh Dad?"

"Yes, pretty cool, but not surprising," Ted laughed. "You know the old saying, right? 'Olive oil is thicker than blood.'"

"He made that up, girls. You're terrible, Teddy."

"Well, what if I did? It was a long time ago, so it is *old*," Ted offered in his own defense.

"Leave the man alone, I like it," Marie added.

"You like *him*," Liz kidded.

"What if I do? He seems like a good guy....for a damn Greek," Marie countered with a smile as she downed another glass of Sicilian red.

By this time Ted was well into the frivolity everyone else was enjoying, and he was going with the flow with a vengeance. Waving his hand in a sweeping, circular motion to indicate he was speaking to all those assembled, he grabbed a glass, filled it with Metaxa, stood up, and made an impromptu but impassioned speech.

"Ladies, raise your glasses. I propose a toast to good people, good friends, and the islands off of Italy and Greece – with a special bravo to the six lovely women assembled here. OPA! How about some coffee and dessert – cannolis and baklava?"

Teddy got the coffee while his wife and daughter brought out some cannolis, baklava, and other assorted Italian and Greek treats. It had certainly been quite an evening between the new friends, the island connection, and a half-century reunion!., As long as the "plate dropper" had the floor and a drink, he decided to keep going, which was all right with the "gentler" sex, as all of them were busy with their coffee and selecting something sweet to finish off their meal.

"One thing I've learned is that you never know what each

day will bring. It's like a pitcher making a pitch – fastball, curve, ball or strike, swing or take. Just like baseball," Ted concluded – at least for the time being.

"If you couldn't tell, my husband is partial to baseball, especially the Dodgers," Gina threw in, giving Ted a hug.

"The Mets for my husband," Marie added proudly.

"Yankees for mine," Marica said with a wistful look.

"How long are you ladies staying? The season opens up in a couple of weeks. We could all go to a game," Ted said hopefully.

"Just a week for the Greek sisters," Mable answered.

"Same for the Sicilians," Marie added.

"Too bad. You really need more than a week to see California."

"Well, all we got is a week, My nephew gave us this as a Christmas present," Mable explained.

"Yeah, same here. My niece gave us a week as well," Liz added. And before the obvious question was asked, Marie finished up: "Yup, for Christmas."

"Wow, that was really nice of them," Teddy observed.

"Yeah, it was," Mable jumped in. "But I think they just wanted to get rid of us, right Marie?"

Marie laughed and nodded and laughed some more.

"You don't mean they pulled a fast one on you guys? Where would that personality trait come from, huh?" Teddy deadpanned, looking right at Mable. "But I think we might be missing the big picture, here..."

Christina and her mother looked at each other. Gina rolled her eyes as she half shrugged, smiled, and said: "Here we go. Here we go."

Apparently, Ted had to deal with this attitude before. Actually, thousands of times before, so he was used to his wife and daughter poo-pooing his ideas.

"Scoff if you will, but I think something bigger than all of us is at work here. Look at the facts: we've got four 'good friends' who just met because their "child" just happened to give them the same Christmas present and booked them on the same flight, and, of all the places to eat you could have chosen, you wind up in a place run by a Greek, a Cephalonian, and a Sicilian, and...."

"Oh my God," Mable interjected, "my daughter called us and recommended this restaurant."

Everyone stopped and looked around at each other as if they were expecting someone's head to go spinning around or to turn into a spirit and fly off. Perhaps they did, but, just for the record, no one's body, or body parts didbanything supernatural.

"And of course we have the 'Cephalonian Reunion,' Gina added. "Yeah, Ted, I think this time you might be onto something," as she gave him a quick kiss.

The four travelers were slightly overwhelmed by the events of the last twenty-four hours. They were also stuffed to the gills, and a bit more than *three* sheets to the proverbial wind.

Marie had yet to divulge the story behind her distrust of her daughter and Nick, which had been triggered by their phone conversations, but she was still convinced that the trip, while gracious and generous, was a way of getting her and Liz out of the way for a while. She gave the group a quick synopsis of what her suspicions were, and why she had them.

Oddly, it was not Mable but Marica, the "intellectual," who spoke first.

"You know, you might be right, Marie, when you said they were sending us here to get rid of us. I mean, my son is not bad, as kids go, but he rarely has been considerate or acceded to what I wanted. Then, out of the blue, he comes up with the Christmas present of all time. I think he might have just wanted to get me and my sister out of commission for a while, so he wouldn't feel guilty about all the things he did, and never did."

All the mothers at the table nodded and nodded and nodded.

"Well, my daughter's gonna get a piece of my mind tomorrow," Marie vociferously exclaimed. "And if I ever find out there was something going on with her and that damn Greek she works with, watch out!" And then, looking at the Greek sisters and Ted as well, she quickly added – "uh, no offense intended."

"None taken," Ted replied. "What a story you guys are living. You should write a book about it, People would love it...."

"And that's another thing, she and that damn teacher she works with are writing a book together. It's supposed to be about teaching, but I can just imagine what it's really about."

Suddenly a light went off in Marica's head, as she asked matter-of-factly.

"Marie, where does your daughter teach?"

"Uh," Marie stuttered as the brandy was impacting her sense of anything. "She teaches at....uh....Liz, where the hell does Maria teach?"

Her sister smiled. "Burns High School."

Marica jumped in with the follow-up. "Oh my goodness.! That's where my son teaches. Maybe they know each other. Did she ever mention a teacher named Nick, Nick Pappas?"

Marie almost choked on her coffee, as she gulped and coughed and spit it out all over the table...."Know each other? Know each other?, He's the one who's writing the damn book with her...and doing God knows what else." Then she caught the glare in Marica's eyes...."Well, at least thinking about doing God knows what else."

"Listen, I know my son. He treats me like garbage sometimes, but he is a family man and a perfect gentleman. And I resent any insinuations to the contrary."

Mable, of all people, was the calmest and became, as it were, the peacemaker and voice of reason. "You know what I think, I think that they got together and gave us these trips just to get us out of their hair, and to get us thinking and supposing just to drive us crazy. My nephew is not a bad guy, but he is sneaky. And Marica, don't get mad – I know he's married with a lot of kids, but he does like the opposite sex, and he always has. And he does like to tease people and flirt with beautiful women. That is part of who he is. A big part!" She looked over at her sister, who grudgingly nodded and sighed. Mable had a head of steam, and continued with her analysis, as everyone else listened intently. "And that book – about teaching? I don't think so. I think they're writing a book about us, about how horrible we are and how much we put them through their whole lives. They see a chance to get even, and they're taking it."

A hush of agreement fell over the crowd, as her "treatise" got an A+ from all concerned.

"We are in the presence of greatness, here," Ted finally said. "When the queen of practical jokes gives her analysis, that's it, brother. That's it."

The puzzle seemed to have been if not solved, at least parsed out into pieces, and the tension was broken. The good time became even better.

"How about it Ladies, one more quick round?" Ted buzzed, as he waved to a passing waiter/ Everyone soon had a fresh glass and a new outlook both on themselves and their friends, "Let's each propose a toast to mark this night of nights.... Christina, why don't you lead off...."

"To family."

"To my incorrigible husband," Gina put in.

"To new friends," Liz said with a smile.

"To Sicilians....and Greeks," from Marie.

"To stories yet untold," added Marica.

"To finding a new life ...and living it.... Ted said with simple sincerity.

"To old friends and new schemes," Mable concluded, as they all downed their drinks in one shot.

CHAPTER TWENTY-ONE

Problems by Any Other Name

...An Email Between Neighbors

To: Npappas@bhs.org

From: Morlando@bhs.org

Re: What the hell is going on

Nick had barely gotten home when he noticed the light on his computer indicating a new email. Probably the best thing to do would have been to ignore it. It was late and he was gassed, but Nick had a thing about messages, Whether it was a voicemail, a text, or an email, he had to check repeatedly to see who was trying to tell him what. So he flipped up the screen and read the rather frantic and cryptic message from Maria. The whole text was only slightly longer than the subject line.

"GREEK...WHAT THE HELL IS GOING ON?"

For once in his life Nick was succinct and also pretty much on the mark with his reply:

"Maria – I think they just want to have an adventure. Get some sleep. We'll talk at school OK? Don't worry....love ya, Greek."

"Thanks, man. I needed that. G'night."

Believe it or not, Nick was correct: the ladies were about to embark on an adventure that would include themselves, Maria and Nick, and actually quite a few others. But no one could imagine the roller coaster ride they were about to undertake!

The morning came much too quickly. It usually does under even normal circumstances, but after teaching a whole day, going through College Night, and then dealing with whatever was going on in Los Angeles, both Maria and Nick were pretty well beat to shit, to quote a popular and very fitting phrase. Nick's mind was on the events and implications of the previous evening and wasn't paying full attention to the road ahead, which was at that moment being crossed by three rather large deer. He looked up barely in time to swerve out of the way, and he forced himself to focus on his driving and not on what might or might not have been going on with their relatives. Of course, there were other items of concern. He was worried about Maria, who was normally a rock when it came to emotional matters, but who seemed both concerned and shaken up by what had transpired. He liked her a lot (no kidding) and he genuinely didn't want to see her hurt or upset, but being honest, he had a hard time interacting with his lunch partner even when she was in a good mood. When she became "pensive" (read "moody") – watch out.

He didn't remember driving the rest of the way to school, but apparently, he had done so because the next thing he saw was the big, gray building that housed his place of employment. "Holy crap, school," he said half out loud, as he turned the corner toward the parking lot. Nick tried to think of what he'd be doing with his various classes, but he drew a big fat blank. Hopefully, once he got to his desk, a glance at his lesson plans would kick his mind into gear. As he drove down the long sloping driveway to the parking spaces, he glanced into the rearview mirror and had to look twice more to be sure his sleepy eyes weren't playing tricks on him. It was Maria. She *always* beat him to school by at least a quarter-hour; her car was always there first. "Wow," he reasoned, she must be worried about her mom and aunt – and maybe herself.

Nick pulled into an empty spot and Maria parked right next to him. He walked over to the driver's side as she was pulling down the window.

"I don't know about you, Nick, but these College Nights really knock me out. It's like teaching two days in one."

"Yeah, you and me both. I'm gassed, and that's an understatement," Nick contributed, all the while shaking his head.

"Well, luckily they're having class meetings for the first hour, so we can just drop off our homerooms and then catch our breath a bit," she added.

"Class meetings! I forgot all about them." Nick breathed a sigh of relief. "Yeah. It will give me time to figure out what I'm going to do today. Is that why you got in later than usual? I was kind of worried about you after last night with your Mom."

"It's definitely been on my mind – most of the night. You wanna meet for coffee after we drop our classes off? My Mom was acting mighty strange, even for her. She said they were kicking up their heels with two Greek ladies? Who were they? Wait, I think I talked with one of them. Named Mable."

Suddenly Maria's face became a bit more solemn as she turned and looked directly at Nick. "Yes, Mable....!

"That's my aunt's name, Maria...Mable!! I thought you had said that last night, but everything was so jumbled I wasn't sure I heard you right."

"Nick, you don't suppose that our moms and aunts met up

with each other? Is that possible?"

Nick's countenance took on a serious, incredulous tone.

"But if it is my mother and aunt, it would mean they met on the plane and all of a sudden became dinner partners? How could that be? Maybe it's someone else, and the name is just a coincidence. There are probably thousands of Greeks in LA. It could very well be other Greeks. Or...maybe it is my relatives, and they all wound up at the same restaurant, and then were thrown together because it was so crowded. Isn't that a possibility?" He kept thinking out loud and clutching at straws as they walked up the stairs to the entrance to the school. "But I have a sinking feeling that they did meet on the plane and somehow hit it off. Could that have really happened? Lord, what have we done?"

"What do you mean 'we,' Nick?" Maria shot back. "I had booked this trip six months ago. When did you arrange yours? This is your fault, you frickin' Greek."

Things had gotten a bit out of hand, which could have been due to the lack of sleep for both the antagonists and the pressure of not knowing what was transpiring three thousand miles west and three hours later. But, truth be told, both Maria and Nick were hot-blooded to say the least, and every once in a while their vitriolic nature came bursting to the surface. They continued their "discussion" as they walked into the hallway, already populated by a few dozen students, several of whom turned toward the two animated teachers.

"Trouble in paradise, Mr. Pappas?" kidded one senior boy whom Nick had known for many years. His comment actually snapped Nick back to a semblance of reality. He stopped short and turned to face Maria.

"Sorry. Didn't mean to go off on you. Lots of stuff going on and my brain cells need a cup of coffee.

"Yeah, no big deal, Nick," she answered. "We can relax a bit and sort this out while the classes are meeting. OK?"

"Sounds good," Nick replied sincerely.

But things were about to get more complicated as another sound came cascading through the halls. It was the principal with an announcement.

"This is Mr. Morgan. Due to circumstances beyond our control, the class meetings have been postponed for today. We will follow the normal schedule for Tuesday. I repeat: class meetings canceled, normal Tuesday schedule. Have a good day."

"Shit!" Nick exclaimed, probably too loud.

"YUP!" Maria added. "Catch you at lunch, man...."

CHAPTER TWENTY-TWO

A Long Day

It was one of those days that should happen to someone else. Nick couldn't find the movie he was going to show to his first class, the principal stopped in "just to say Hi," and his mother and aunt were on his mind, especially the possibility that they had met Maria's relatives. God knows what they would be saying about him and her if that turned out to be the case. He thought about calling their hotel, but given the time difference it was too early to do that, and by the time lunch duty rolled around he was beside himself with worry, stress, and, yes, GUILT.

He and Maria got into the cafeteria at the same time, and she was literally fuming. He could almost see the smoke coming out of her head, and he *could see*, literally, the sparks flying out of her eyes. Today there were no prelims, no warming up – she started right in.

"So I call out there, and my mother doesn't answer her phone. Then I call the goddamn hotel, and they tell me she and my aunt are out. It's nine in the morning there – where the hell could they be going at nine in the morning? Something's not right. Something is up. Hi, Nick."

"Hey, Maria. Yeah, it's like they've disappeared off the face of the earth. I mean, we know they got there all right, and my aunt did call her daughter, but it's not like my mother not to let *me* know. I feel helpless. And guilty. Come to think of it, that's more or less how I felt during most of my life. Holy smokes...."

Just at that moment the principal and vice-principal walked in, but there must have been something else on their minds since they walked by the two teachers without so much as a perfunctory greeting, which was fortunate, because the mood Nick was in his reply would have probably been unprintable.

Maria had that look about her that told Nick she was about to add something important to their discussion, so perhaps the brief interruption by the two administrators was a blessing, as it were.

"Nick, I think that might be it."

"What might be it?"

"GUILT, you idiot. GUILT! They've been doing this to us our whole lives, and this situation is perfect for them....Guilt from a distance. Get it? They are still controlling us and making us feel guilty. Having said that, I am worried about them all, and, yes, I feel guilty, damn it. Damn it Greek."

Nick could only nod in agreement and shake his head in despair. She was right. Guilt was such a powerful weapon, especially when practiced by Mediterranean mothers. But, to paraphrase an old axiom, they hadn't seen nothing yet! It was one thing to have done something, or not done something, and pay the consequences. It's like a little kid getting punished for a transgression he didn't commit, or for a misstep from so long ago, it was forgotten. Well, the seeds of Maria and Nick's guilt had been planted when they were both very young and nurtured to their current insidious level throughout their lives. But the genesis of their current confusion and worry had been devised and implemented in the previous twenty-four hours, as these clever ladies concocted a plan to throw their kids the ultimate curve ball!

CHAPTER TWENTY-THREE

Wednesday Morning
Calming Down

Tuesday went by without a word, or call, or text, or email – nothing from the four wayward women. Maria texted Nick first thing in the morning: "Still no word. How about you? Worried."

"Ditto" was his succinct and pithy response.

The blank stares that each of the two teachers wore into their encounter at lunchtime indicated that neither one of them had heard or seen anything Trying to add a little levity to what was becoming – despite the poo-pooing from both of them – a worrisome situation, Nick, as was his wont, said something he shouldn't have.

"Maybe your mother was right. Maybe you should go to confession. Maybe we should both go," he offered with a forced smile.

Maria was not in the mood.

"What the hell are you talking about? Greeks don't go to confession."

"Just trying to lighten things up a bit...sorry, Maria."

"Don't worry about it," she replied. "I'm just edgy."

The lunch period rolled along, and the weather was surprisingly "springy," and unexpected for a day in mid-March. Many of the students took advantage of the sunshine and were eating outside at the picnic tables, which was fine with Maria and Nick since that meant fewer kids to watch. In actuality, they weren't paying much attention to any of the students, due to their preoccupation with their "missing" relatives.

"I just wish we'd hear something, anything," Nick blurted out after a long timeout from speaking, or doing much of anything at all. He probably wished he could have taken that statement back, as almost on cue he got an email, not from his mother or aunt, but from his mother's bank, where she and Nick had a joint account. It was to let him know that $10,000 had been transferred to a company account in California. He almost fell out of his seat, and it was all he could do to grab his partner's arm and point to the screen.

"MARIA! LOOK! Ten big ones. What the hell?"

Now, this was really his mother's account, and it was her money. Nick's name was on it for convenience and emergencies. But the question was, why would she transfer all that money?

"Nick, why would she transfer all that money?" Maria repeated, as if she had read his mind.

"That's what I was just asking myself??"

Just then Maria got a text. It was from her mother. Short and to the point: "CHK YR LPTP." She flipped up her screen and turned to email. There was one line of text – "THIS IS WHERE WE'RE STAYING," – and an attachment. Maria shot an elbow into Nick's side to get his attention. It would have done an NBA player proud.

"Nick, look at this...!!! Look at this....!!!"

The attachment contained a picture of the four smiling sisters standing in an elegant-looking yard with a pool, beautiful grounds, and a path leading down to the beach and the ocean. The Pacific Ocean!

"WHAT THE... Nick began to exclaim, but Maria shot a hand quickly over his mouth before he could finish. But her eyes were on fire with surprise and bewilderment, and they were both beside themselves, figuratively and literally. Holy Cow!!

CHAPTER TWENTY-FOUR

California Girls

The stories and laughter and eating and drinking continued long into the night, and the four Jersey girls were a bit worn out after their travels, both physically and metaphorically. Gina asked them if they had anything planned for the morrow. The day after a long trek is often more tiring than the first, and the four senoras had planned to sit and relax on a bus tour which had apparently been part of their vacation package. She looked over at her husband who was already shaking his head.

"Bus tour? I don't think so. We've been out here for thirty years, and we know "what's what" more than anyone else, tour or no tour. Why would you want to sit on a crowded bus when you can have two willing and eager servants at your beck and call? We can see the sights, eat the food, and take in the most beautiful part of this beautiful state. I'll bring our big and comfortable SUV, loaded with great songs, and with you – great people."

"Absolutely, Ladies. We won't take no for an answer," Gina added. "Like Ted said, we know the sights, and we also know the people. A lot of the 'celebrities' have been eating here for years and they've become our friends. Maybe you'd like to meet a few. I know they'd like to meet you!! And, oh yeah, wear something casual and comfortable!"

Mable and Marie jumped at the offer, notwithstanding Marie's comment to her sister about "Greeks bearing gifts." Liz said it sounded OK to her, too, but Marica, the studious thinker, was hesitant, saying that they didn't want to disrupt the couple's lives or put them out at all. But Ted, insisted, threatening to hold them hostage in the diner until they agreed to his offer. So it became a done deal! Gina and Ted drove them to their hotels, and indicated they would see them around nine in the morning.

"Get some rest, ladies, and get ready for a great day!"

Ted and Gina were as good as their word – they were at the ladies' hotels right at nine, just as they said they would be. Despite the seemingly exorbitant amount of alcohol they had consumed, none of them appeared to be hungover, which was astounding. In fact, they all felt great. Go figure....Anyway, it looked like it was going to be a glorious day weather wise, The sun was bright and beaming, and the temperature was supposed to hit the upper sixties. What could be better?

They stopped at *ITALIANS AND GREEKS* for breakfast, a "working breakfast" if you will to map out their day. After they were seated and coffee was served all around, Ted excused himself for a few moments.

"Something I said?" the younger Greek sister asked, as she fixed her coffee and took that all-important first sip.

Marie nudged Mable. "Your sister is starting to loosen up! That's good!"

"That's dangerous!" Mable kidded.

"My husband didn't mean to be rude. He thinks he makes the greatest pancakes in the world. He'll be back shortly!"

He was back quicker than anyone expected, carrying four orders of pancakes at once, with no hint of smashing any of the plates, and he couldn't resist taking a shot at his adversary from the old country.

"I was going to see if these were 'magic plates' and drop them, but I thought I'd better not risk it." he smiled. Mable stuck her tongue out and cocked her head.

He distributed the plates with the hotcakes steaming and giving off an aroma of home and good eating. Gina looked quizzically at her husband.

"Yes, dear, I'll be right back with ours!" he quipped as he headed back to the kitchen.

"These are absolutely delicious!" Liz began. "How in the world did he make them so quickly?"

"Don't tell my husband I told you this," Gina confessed, "but he always makes the batter the night before, and he had one of the cooks heat up the griddle before we came in."

"However he does it, these are out of this world," Marie added, in between bites and sips of coffee. "Out of this world!!"

Ted was back with plates for himself and his wife and a big smile, which seemed to .be a permanent fixture on his broadly handsome face. Marica made a complimentary re-mark about his disposition.

"Your hotcakes are a hit, Ted!" Gina informed him.

"Well, aren't they always?," he replied.

"And he's modest, too," Gina remarked.

Ted had barely sat down to take a sip of coffee when he stood right back up.

"Will you excuse me for a moment? I forgot to tell the cook about a luncheon party I had booked. Be right back." On his way, he tapped their waitress on the shoulder and pointed to the table.

"More coffee coming up, boss," she said pleasantly.

"Your daughter's not working this morning?," Mable asked.

"No, she's actually in college, at UCLA. I urged her to take a business course, but she wants to be a writer. There's so much competition, you know?"

Marica scrunched her face up and shook her head vigorously. "I know exactly what you mean; just like my son. He got a good teaching job and he says to me he really wants to be a writer. I told him to stick to what he was good at! There are thousands of people who want to be writers....with nothing to show for it but disappointment!"

"Just like my Maria," Marie added. "She's a great teacher, and even though her salary's not great, it pays the bills. But I know she's always wanted to do something else, too."

The mothers' symposium came to a halt when Ted returned carrying what looked like a bunch of travel brochures. He put them down next to his plate, had a swig of coffee, and took a big mouthful of hotcakes. He looked around at the Jersey girls with an expectant expression filling his face and the hotcakes filling his mouth.

Gina spoke up for everyone.

"Yes, dear, the reviews are in, and everyone loved the flapjacks."

Gina knew her husband. He couldn't have started his days without some praise for his breakfast, and he also couldn't stand the term flapjacks. She loved to see him smile and cringe at the same time (a reaction Nick often elicited from Maria, though in Nick's case it was unintentional).

"So, dear, where do we take this fearsome foursome on their first full day in paradise?"

Ted turned toward his wife, with a mouthful of coffee and was so anxious to get his thoughts out that he swallowed it while it was still a bit on the steamy side. Everyone chuckled as the slightly scalded host laughed at himself with a self-deprecating comment. "Well, I've always told my wife that I'm hot...."

It wasn't easy to calm himself down. Like most Italians and

Greeks, laughing uncontrollably was an intrinsic part of Ted's personality, and he felt that the best laughs are the ones at your own expense.

"Whew. Sorry ladies. I always said there's nothing like a good cup of coffee to get you going in the morning. OK, speaking of going....we, Gina and I, were talking last night, and there's no way you're going back to Jersey in one week. There's just not enough time to see all there is to see and meet all the people you'd love to meet."

Gina, sensing that their guests were somewhat "surprised" by her husband's comment, shook her head emphatically and "saved" him, which she had done countless times over the years of their marriage.

"What my talk first and think later husband meant, was, is that we'd love to have you stay out here longer, and we feel we've got a plan that you might like to consider."

"Thanks, Gina. What would I do without you?" Ted stated sincerely.

"The question is what am I to do *with* you?"

Ted smiled, gave his wife a quick hug, and began passing out the booklets he had brought to the table. A dealer in Vegas or Atlantic City couldn't have done it any smoother.

"I still have the good hands," he said, complimenting his own dexterity. "I think I could still play some shortstop if I wanted to..."

"...if you do say so yourself," his wife added, completing his thought with a chuckle. "Could you please just tell the girls what we discussed and save the self praise for later?"

The ladies had picked up their booklets and were immersed in the pictures and descriptions they contained.

"What a beautiful place this is," Liz began.

"This is all one city?" Marie asked with just a touch of awe.

"I think I've heard of this," Marica added. "Montecito, yeah, I've read about it."

"Is it as good as it looks?" Mable wondered.

"You'll soon see for yourselves, cause that's where we're headed. If that's OK with you that is," Gina asked semi-rhetorically

"It sounds wonderful! Marie exclaimed.

"If my son could see where we're about to go," Rica exclaimed loudly.

Ted thought he should fill in the blanks as they finished their coffee.

"Well, it's one of the most exquisite and exclusive places in the USA, actually, in the whole world. The list of celebrities who live there would knock you out – yet many of them are regulars here and we've become good friends. They hold their annual fundraiser at our restaurant, and the booklets you're looking at were an offshoot of one of the dinners. Melissa Topping came up with the idea. Perhaps you've heard of her?"

"Yes. She's on TV, right?" Mable asked.

"Yeah, Melpo, she's the hostess of that show uh, what's it called?" Marie threw in.

"*IT'S NEVER TOO LATE,*" Liz said excitedly. "Right?"

"Would you like to meet her?"

"Sure, I've seen her, she's very smart," Rica said sincerely.

"And she's very nice as well, I listed her house," Gina stated matter of factly.

Everyone turned their heads in slight bewilderment.

"You did what?" Liz asked.

"Yeah, I'm a realtor part-time. I love it, and I got to get away from Ted sometimes, right dear?" she chided her husband, who smiled and shook his head. "It's not easy being married to a Cephalonian!"

"Don't we know it?" Marica and Mable said almost in unison. "Don't we know it!"

Everyone was in an expectant mood, eager to see the things Ted and Gina had been talking about, so they finished up their last sips of coffee and headed outside. All the ladies commented on how gorgeous the weather was. Ted smiled and shrugged: "Just another day in California."

The SUV was sparkling in and out. I looked like it had just been washed and polished, and it was roomy and comfortable. Marie and Mable took the back seats, Marica and Liz in the middle, with Gina riding shotgun. Ted slipped a CD into the slot, and they were all set.

"Hope you like the music. It's a variety of songs, all easy to listen to; I'll keep it low. Are we all set?" Ted looked back at his guests, who indicated everything was good.

"Talk is cheap, Ted. Let's go." his wife chided.

As they drove they were greeted by breathtaking views of the mountains, the beach, and the heavenly sun. Ted opened the sunroof and windows, and the gentle, cooling breeze was like a welcome mat beckoning the ladies to enjoy themselves. And were they ever enjoying themselves? Conversations were humming all over the car, covering everything: what they saw out the windows; how this whole adventure came about; what their kids would say if they could see them; the "feel" of being here and experiencing this place and these people. And there were questions for Gina and Ted about them, about their business, and especially about this fabulous part of the country. It was almost like a trip back to the 'old country: ("countries"), which all four of them desired but probably knew deep inside that they would never take. Their fanciful pipe dream was about to be reinforced by Ted the "tour guide"...

"You know, this part of the state was once a hideout for highwaymen, who robbed the people going from one town to another. But by the latter third of the 1800s the gangs were gone and a large number of immigrants from Italy began to settle here."

Marie poked Mable gently in the ribs.

"See, Italians know a good thing when they see it."

"They probably felt at home with the climate and coast, huh?" Liz added.

"Absolutely," Gina said. "This reminded them very much of Italy, and they grew produce as they used to do back home. And today this is one of the garden spots of not only California, but of the world, if you'll pardon the pun."

"Montecito! Can't beat it," Ted re-emphasized. "How about a look at the beach?"

They had been going for well over an hour, and a stretch of the legs, and the rest of the torso, seemed like a good idea to all parties. Ted pulled the car over and parked under a small grove of trees adjacent to one of the most beautiful stretches of sand one could imagine, with a stone wall just begging to be used for a natural seat and table. The word "idyllic" would have been a huge understatement, and the panoramic view left the ladies speechless, which was really saying something given their propensity for conversing with each other. The sound of the surf gently lapping onto the pristine sand evoked more emotions and memories than the sisters could count, and the aromatic scent of the ocean brought back other days and times, hidden hopes and secret wishes...

"I just love the ocean," Liz remarked. "I guess it's in my blood."

"Me, too, me, too." Mable agreed. " It is so relaxing." She seemed very subdued and pensive.

"It's who we are," Marie stated on behalf of all the sisters. "It's where we're from, The islands will always be a part of us!"

For her part, Marica just stared out at the Pacific, lost in thought.

Somehow a quaint picnic basket had manifested itself and was sitting invitingly on the sand....

"My husband *never* goes anywhere without 'provisions,'" Gina explained.

Ted just shrugged.

"Thought everyone could use something to snack on," he said, faking a defensive demeanor. "Just some iced espresso, oranges, almonds, and biscotti. How does that sound?"

"Damn good," Marica emphatically stated. "Damn good!"

Mable looked at Marie as her eyes widened almost to her ears.

Both Sicilians looked at Rica in disbelief. Who was this woman??

Gina took everything in stride and put things in perspective with her straightforward and sincere observation: "That's what Montecito can do to you, especially if you're Mediterranean."

"That's right," Ted added. "We came here for a vacation thirty years ago, and we never left..." He looked around at the four ladies. "Maybe the same thing will happen to you."

The sets of sisters became very pensive after his last comment, and the lull became almost eerie. Once again it was Gina to the rescue.

"Girls, if I can get your mind off what my husband said for just a moment, I have something else for you to wrap your heads around. But first, have a piece of fruit and a biscotti, and a few sips of coffee. Look At this marvelous setting, eat, drink, and relax!"

The ladies dutifully did as Gina directed, and before long they were their old selves again, no pun intended. Marie broke the ice with the question in everyone's thoughts.

"OK, Gina, from one Sicilian to another, what exactly was it you wanted us to 'wrap our heads around'?"

Gina cocked her head and grinned..

"What you think, Gina? We can't wrap our minds around what you're gonna say?" Mable threw in, half in jest.

"I agree with my Greek compatriot," Liz added in support.

"Yeah, Gina, spit it out, dammit," Rica interjected. "What

the hell is on your mind?" The "new" Marica seemed to have taken hold. Was this who she really was? Was it the bottled-up hostility coming out? It was like a bombshell! As Mable whispered to Marie: "My sister never was Pollyanna. She didn't hide her tough side, but I've never seen her like this! I wonder what my nephew would say?"

Mable was about to apologize for her sister, but Gina waved her off.

"Hey, that's a great lead into what I was going to say. Have some of the refreshments and think about what has transpired over the last day or so. It's about eleven-thirty, give or take, which means yesterday, twenty-four hours ago, it was about two thirty Jersey time. You were flying across the country. Now, less than twenty-four hours later, you're in a different place, with new friends – four of them I hope – (she pointed to herself and her husband), new feelings, new opportunities. But you're all still you." She noticed the puzzled looks on their faces and tried to address their confusion.

"I need two more sentences, OK?"

The ladies all nodded....

"I've heard you talk about a great number of things, including your ethnicity, your beliefs, your emotions – but mostly about the heartache of being mothers." She held up one finger for that sentence. "Why don't you put all your thoughts into a book and tell people what it's really like being who you are??" Two fingers from Gina.

"Yeah, why not?" Marie asked. "Our kids are writing one; let's beat them to the punch!"

"You mentioned that last night, but I thought you were just making conversation," Liz added.

"I was dead serious then, and even more serious now," Gina emphatically replied.

"A great idea," Mable contributed loudly. "A great idea. What do you think, Marica?"

"Best damn idea I ever heard!"

It was unanimous, Ted included.

"I can't wait to see this," he beamed.

"But how do we get started?" Marie wondered.

Gina's face lit up as she held up a small gray device about four inches square. It was an old-fashioned, portable cassette recorder. She explained what it was and that she and Ted always kept it in the car to record ideas for the restaurant and slogans to use when pitching a house. Sometimes, she indicated, she would just record her thoughts about...well....whatever she was thinking about.

"Pretty clever, Gina!" Liz remarked.

"Well, I have to tip my hat to Christina for this. She always carries a recorder with her to preserve ideas she gets for her writing." Gina paused as if she were hesitant to go one.

"And..." Rica prompted.

"Well, I have a small confession. I've had it on all morning, and I got just about everything you said. I thought that might make a good start. Am I forgiven?"

The grins all around were her answer.

"It's tough trying to keep up with this Sicilian of mine!" Ted smiled, as he gave his wife a big kiss. "But I agree with her totally on this. I think you guys could come up with a book that would put your feelings on the map. Christina already told us that she would help edit it if you would like. How could you miss?"

Everyone was all in, but Rica did have a caveat: "But when can we get this done?"

Marie agreed. "Yeah, we only have a week here, and we would like to see some more of California. Is it possible?"

"Maybe our lunch date will clear some of these things up and put your minds at ease. There are a couple more things I'd like you to see on the way. So just relax and take in the sights and feel of this beautiful day. They're expecting us in about a half hour or so, and I think my timing is pretty good. OK?"

"You gotta trust Ted on this one," Gina quipped as she turned the recorder back on. "All aboard, ladies!"

CHAPTER TWENTY-FIVE

Lunch with a Celebrity

The sisters were energized by the realization that they could do something to make their feelings known, but also that what they were about to embark upon would be a total blindside for their kids, and for everyone else they knew. The next half hour or so was very relaxing, as their "tour" showcased the beauty and grandeur of this garden of eden like place they had stumbled upon. They talked quite a bit, but the tone was low key and light as their vacation took yet one more unexpected turn. Both Mable and Marie felt that there was some other hand guiding their journey and easing them into what could only be described as heaven in every respect.

They wound around a number of quaint, picturesque streets with all different houses and landscapes. It was awesome and inspiring, and it provided a tranquility that perfectly blended with their mood. Ted pulled the car down a one lane street called Hillside Road, which was quite appropriate since it seemed to climb quickly up into the summit of the surrounding area.

"There's the house," Gina pointed out.

A narrow, winding walkway consisting of a variety of stones led up to the door. Beautiful ferns, trees, and other lush vegetation guarded either side of the walk. Mable got out of the car and was transfixed by the picture in front of her.

"What's the matter, Melpo?" Marie asked with just a bit of concern. "Are you all right?"

"Yeah, yeah, I'm fine. It's just that this reminds me of our village in Greece. It looks exactly the same. Marica was too young when we left, but I remember it like it was yesterday. It's like going back in time."

"This is what the towns in Sicily look like, too, from the pictures I've seen. Something or someone brought us to this place, Mable," Marie added with a bittersweet smile.

They hugged several times, and then realized there were other people viewing their nostalgic journey. But there were no worries. The ladies all were fighting back tears, and Ted made a comment about the sea air affecting his eyes. Gina clicked off the recorder, and motioned for everyone to come up to the front door.

"How about a picture, ladies, with the house in the background," Gina asked as she indicated a good place to stand. The sisters were all smiles, and they wound up posing for several shots: hugging, waving at the house, with arms spread to show the magnitude of their location. They took some with all six of them; separate ones of the two sets of sisters, Mable and Ted, Gina and Ted...it was glorious. No one noticed the front door being opened, or the comely, smiling woman standing there taking it all in. It was their host, Melissa Reynolds.

"I hope you know I charge a pretty penny for using my house as a backdrop!" she jokingly said, as she walked out to hug Gina and then Ted. "So, these must be the 'fabulous females,' you were telling me about at one this morning! Let's see if I can guess who's who!"

She batted a thousand as she pointed at each of the women

and called out their names: "Liz, Marie, Mable, Marica. Right?"

"Perfect Liss," Ted beamed.

"How'd you do that?" Marie wondered.

"Hey, you don't get our own show without learning a few tricks along the way," she admitted.

For her part, Gina swatted her husband hard on the back of his head.

"What's the matter with you? You called her at one in the morning?"

"Hey, I learned that from you. Strike while the iron is hot and all that other good philosophic advice you're always throwing at me. Well?"

"Yeah, yeah. Sorry, Liss..." Gina sincerely apologized.

"It's fine. The important thing is we're all here. Let's go inside!"

The inside of the house was spacious, yet cozy. There were rooms upon rooms, all decorated with the eye of someone who valued comfort and tradition. The furniture looked as if it might have been in a modest home in the Midwest rather than in a multi-million dollar residence in an exclusive California hillside. There was a room with a solid wall of books – much too lived in to be called a library, and the kitchen seemed to say "have a cup of coffee and stay a while."

"Some place, huh, ladies?" Gina asked rhetorically.

"You are the master of understatements, Gina," Marica offered.

"Some place? SOME PLACE!" Liz added.

"It's such a beautiful day that I had Maria set up lunch outside, If that is OK with everyone," Melissa offered as she opened two French doors.to reveal a vista usually reserved for a movie scene. There was a patio surrounded by lush plants and trees, and a winding path leading down to the beach about a hundred yards away.

"WOW" was written on everyone's face, as they made their

way out toward a rustic-looking picnic table right out of Norman Rockwell. The Pacific provided an elegant backdrop to the scene, and the soft sound of the waves was the perfect musical accompaniment to complete what surely had to be a dream. The table was set with paper plates and plastic utensils, more "picnic-like," their hostess explained.

The housekeeper seemed to know Gina and Ted, rather well, as she hugged the husband and wife and asked how their family was and how things were going at *ITALIANS AND GREEKS*. Ted answered the question on the ladies' minds before they asked.

"Oh yeah, Maria was like a part of our family..."

"You mean 'IS' part of our family," Gina corrected her husband.

"Yes, my wife is right. Maria 'IS' and always will be family. She helped us get our business started many years ago, and then Melissa stole her right out from under us," Ted said jokingly.

"Same name as your daughter, right?" Mable said quietly as she nudged Marie, who just put on a wry smile and nodded.

"Why don't we sit and have something to eat? Ted informed me that you had quite a dinner last night, so Maria prepared a light fare today, if that is OK," Melissa explained.

Apparently the meaning of "light" was different in California than it was in the East. There were platters of olives and cheese, warm chunks of Italian bread, containers of olive oil, tomatoes, and cucumbers, and a large variety of sandwiches cut into convenient triangular pieces, and San Pelligrino water with slices of lemon.

"My goodness, everything looks so delicious, Rica said.

"It sure does," Marie added.

"Please, dig in ladies. My husband really wanted to be here, but he had to go to LA to wrap up a book deal with one of the Dodgers. I told you about that, Ted, right?"

"Yeah, you did. I want an autographed copy, Liss!"

"Book deal?" Liz asked.

"Oh, yeah," Gina answered. "Peter Topping, president of TOP SHELF BOOKS."

"He publishes really interesting stuff with a personal touch," Melissa explained. "One of us has to like the premise before his company will consider it. His latest novel is a best-seller – ACCIDENTAL LOVE."

"Oh, I've heard of that," Rica said, as she took a big bite of bread.

The conversation began to take a back seat to their repast as the ladies began to dig in.

"You know what? We should get a picture of all of us with the ocean in the background."

"Good idea, Mable," Marie chimed in. "Maybe after we eat."

"Our mother used to say if you want to do something, you have to do it when you have the chance. Let's take a couple now, then we can finish, OK?"

"Yeah, let's do it, ladies," Liz agreed.

So, there was a brief intermission in the chewing, and a brief, fun filled picture session. They took every possible combination of people: each set of sisters; the fearsome foursome; Ted and Gina and Melissa; Melissa and the ladies; Maria with each of the combinations....and so on. The smiles were genuine, and when they settled back in to eat, everyone found that their appetites had been spurred by the photo ops!!

In between bites of chicken salad Marie had an epiphany.

"Hey, can I send one of these back to my daughter? It will knock her out!"

"Yes, yes," Mable jumped in. "Send one of the four of us, and tell her this is where we're staying. She'll probably show it to my nephew and they will go nuts!!"

"Well," Melissa began, "there could be more truth than not

in that statement."

"Huh?" Liz wondered

"Let's have coffee and dessert by the pool, and I'll explain the whole thing, if my accomplices (pointing to Ted and Gina) will help fill in the details..."

"We'll not only help with the details, we'll get the coffee and dessert," Ted offered genuinely. "Maria, take some food and take a break for yourself!"

Maria smiled and sat on a lounge chair, stretching and sighing. She smiled and saluted Mr. and Mrs. Micropolis. "You guys are the best."

"We know that!" Ted kidded.

After everyone was settled with coffee and crumb cake, all eyes were on Melissa.

"Ok, it's really pretty simple. We're opening our new season in two weeks, and I need to spend a lot of time in LA. So we're staying at our apartment in the city – it saves a lot of time on the commute, and it would ease things for both my husband and me work-wise and time-wise. Well, Gina was going to rent it out for me, but it's hard to do for that short a period of time, and I don't really like strangers in my house. Maria has a vacation coming up, and I really don't like to leave the house vacant. So...I thought, well, rather Ted suggested, that perhaps the four of you would like to stay here."

Fifty jigsaw puzzles could have been constructed from the looks of astonishment and confusion on the sisters' faces, which caused some chuckles on Ted's part and empathy from Melissa and Gina.

"Ladies, let Ted and me give you a refill and another pinch of cake, and we'll explain, cause I know you must have questions and concerns. Right?"

"First of all, let me say that I think that all this was somehow meant to happen. Yesterday at this time you were just landing at LA X, and I had no idea of what was going to happen. Right??"

They all looked at each other and nodded.

Gina took over. "We've known Melissa for many years. She helped us publicize *ITALIANS AND GREEKS*, and we knew some interesting guests that we got for her show." She waved her hand at Ted, who didn't miss a beat.

"So it all sort of fell into place when we met you all, and it seemed things had come full circle from when I was five. Melissa needed a house-sitter as it were, you guys want some adventure and you have a story to tell – it's a perfect match!"

"But what about the cost?" Marica asked.

"Yeah, we may have gotten loaded last night, but money wise we're not – loaded that is," added Marie.

Melissa couldn't contain her smile.

"Did Ted leave out that there will be no charge for your stay?"

"I thought he said that," Mable replied "Are you sure?"

"Absolutely. BUT – you will owe me something," Liss retorted with a big grin.

"I knew there'd be a catch," Rica said only half seriously. "What is it?"

"You agree to be my first guests for the new season of my show....two weeks from yesterday."

"That's it?" Liz asked.

"Well, we'd also like you to get your thoughts down into a book format....Christina will be on a break from school, and she'd LOVE to come out here and oversee the project," Gina explained.

"Well, everything sounds good, and you people are so nice....but what about our hotels?" Liz asked.

"The two managers are good customers and good friends. I called them while I was supposedly talking to my head chef this morning. If you decide to do this, they will move your reservations up two weeks, no charge, and my wife and I will see to it that you see whatever parts of this state that you'd like to see – at your service as a chauffeur and tour guide." Ted concluded with a huge bow, receiving an ovation from the seven ladies!

"Groceries will be delivered, the liquor cabinet is well stocked, and there will be a car here at your disposal if you'd like to go exploring! Do we have a deal?" Melissa earnestly stated as she bowed to the assembled sisters.

There were smiles and hugs all around, and too many "thank-you's" to record.

"Oh, Melissa, Mable had mentioned this before.. would you be able to send a picture to my daughter, with the caption: 'Look at where we're staying?'" Marie asked. "That will really throw them, right Mable, right Rica?" The Greek sisters high-fived the Sicilians, Gina included.

"Sure thing Marie. Maria is our resident computer expert – could you tell her where we can send it?" Melissa replied.

"Ou, ou," Marica shouted. "I have an idea that will really play with their brains. I have a joint account with my son, and the woman at the bank is a classmate from college. Gina, can you give me the name of your company? I'll call her and have her send an email to my son that I just withdrew ten thousand dollars and forwarded it to you. Combined with the picture, Nick and Maria will have to think it's for rent money, or maybe even a down payment! I'll have her send it during the day when he is at school, and he and Maria can chew on that for a while!!"

"I'm proud of you, Marica. You're starting to think like me!!" Mable said with gusto!

Another round of high fives was followed by some wine and brandy, and an exclamation from Ted: "You guys are something else! I would hate to have you mad at me!"

CHAPTER TWENTY-SIX

The Ladies Write a Book!

MEDITERRANEAN MOTHERS –

THE HEARTACHES & THE TEARS....

LIZ, MARIE, MABLE, MARICA

ACKNOWLEDGEMENTS

Based upon an idea by Gina Micropolis
Edited by Christina Micropolis

PREFACE

We decided to put this volume together because we felt that mothers in general, and Italian and Greek mothers in particular, get a bad rap from the population as a whole, and especially from their selfish, spiteful children.

Let us say right at the outset that while we will bring many of our own experiences into play, this will also be a global compilation of observations and events we have come to know over the cumulative years of our lives.

Who are we? Two sets of widowed sisters, Sicilians (Liz and Marie) and Greeks (Marica and Mable). As of this writing, we have been best friends for exactly seventy-two hours. That's right, just about three days. We met on a flight from New Jersey to LA, and if anyone thinks that things just happen randomly, think again, sister!

DEDICATION

This book is dedicated to mothers everywhere
In the hope that it will help them deal with
Their ungrateful children

INTRODUCTION

We were told by many "experts" that we can't have a PREFACE, a DEDICATION, and an INTRODUCTION. Who cares what they say? This is OUR book, and we'll do as we please.

So, what we'd like you to do is read this as if we were sitting right next to you, and this was more of a conversation between friends – mothers – rather than something to read. Make it personal. At the end of each chapter, we will *pose an opinion question for you on what we said, and a second question relating to your own experiences.*

How does that sound??

Go ahead, let's talk....

CHAPTER 1 – A MOTHER'S LOVE
IS THE ROOT OF ALL HEARTBREAK

Without love we wouldn't care, and if we didn't care, our lives would be a lot easier. I mean a LOT easier. Of course, this is true in other relationships: wives and husbands, siblings, friends. But there is nothing like the love a mother has for her child, and, on the flip side, there is nothing like the heartache, pain, and tears that your children can cause you to feel. There is NOTHING like the pain and emptiness a mother feels, and the reason is very simple: your children were once a part of you. For nine months you get fatter, you are saddled with morning sickness, throw up, can't eat what you want cause nothing tastes good. And then, to top it off, you have the distinct feeling that your lower regions were being ripped apart as the baby is born.

Husbands always say that they love the kids as much as mothers but how can they? They can't possibly have the depth of feelings and hurt that we experience. What exactly is it that they do? They get you pregnant, go about their lives for nine months, and then give out cigars. What a tough role!

And then....diapers, and rashes, and feedings, and baths, and crying, and not sleeping. Husbands make a big deal out of earning the money. Wow, what a sacrifice. That's what they've been doing their whole lives; nothing is different. It's like they go out the door with the attitude..."Well, I gotta go now. Let me know how things turn out." Please...

Q – What do YOU think causes you the most heartbreak?

Q – And, what has your husband done, or not done, that made (or still makes) you furious?

CHAPTER 2 – GETTING OLD STINKS – AND BEING A WIDOW STINKS EVEN MORE

Let's face it, husbands are OK, but they can often be a pain. They never want to do what you want to do, they're on the lazy side at best, and they stick to their old habits as if they were afraid they would run away and leave them. Admittedly, they usually made a decent wage, but if you didn't watch them, they would waste what they earned on non-necessities, often involving some sort of alcoholic beverage or sporting event. Having said that, it was better to have them around from time to time. It was someone to talk to, complain to, threaten the kids with, and correct the behavior of. They were always suckers for the guilt trips we would lay on them, and they rarely if ever saw through our emotional outbreaks usually topped off with a layer of tears. Plus cutting the roast or turkey, taking out the garbage, cutting the lawn, and shoveling snow were all better left to the male of the species.

And where are they now? They all got up and left us, in a manner of speaking. They have died, passed away, whatever term you'd like to use. We feel bad, of course, and we miss them, but being left on your own is no picnic. People look at you and think you are feeble-minded at best and on the brink of kissing your life goodbye. You can tell by the way they look at you and talk to you. Like you're a doddering idiot. And please don't call us "seniors." Seniors are the last year of high school. We find the term very demeaning.

And your kids? You still worry about them, but it seems that they can't grasp what you are going through or what you need. They either suffocate you by making all your decisions or don't get in touch with you for weeks at a time.

> *There's no getting around it, getting old and being a widow is a double whammy we are all cursed with, and having kids is the razor's edge....heartaches and tears!!*
>
> *Q – What is worse, being old, or being a widow?*
> *Q – What would you change about society's view of mothers, young or old?*

The ladies and Christina had been working hard on the manuscript, and they got quite a bit done in one afternoon. They had spent the morning, with Ted and Gina's help, getting all their things together from the hotel and moving into Melissa's house. The whole thing still seemed a bit unbelievable.

"I think you're on the right track, ladies. Keeping it simple and to the point will attract a lot more potential readers and help you get your message across. Rather than being an all-encompassing warehouse of guilt, your book will highlight where you want the reader to go with her thoughts and let them flesh out each chapter with their own experiences and perspectives. Really seems to be working well so far. I think we're on the right track, and I also think we could use a quick coffee break, huh?

"Good idea, Christina. Thanks so much for helping us with this. Your mom's recordings of our conversations gave us a good starting point, and your guidance has been indispensable," Rica began.

"Absolutely," Marie piggy backed. "My daughter is always saying how hard it is to write. It's not really that hard at all, is it?"

"It's not hard when you have the right combination of people doing it. And we have the perfect combination!" Liz added emphatically.

"Damn right," Mable agreed. "Why don't we sit out back. I'll make the coffee"

"I got the snacks, Melpo," Marie volunteered.

Liz and Marica made themselves comfortable in the yard, while Marie and Mable attended to the refreshments. There was a cooling breeze wafting in from the Pacific, and the sun was in its late afternoon glow. Just like a postcard!

"So, what do you think about your new friends, Mable? Do you like us?" Marie said half-jokingly.

"Like you? We love you!!" Mable responded, giving Marie a big hug. "You know, my best friend when I came here from Greece was named Maria, and you're Marie, and your daughter is named Maria, right? Funny how things turn out, huh?"

Christina was in the front yard recording some observations on her recorder. She was truly enjoying doing this project, and she figured she may as well save her thoughts and ideas while they were still fresh. Who knows, she figured, maybe they would provide her with the groundwork for a book of her own someday. She was enjoying working with the women. They were nice people, they had fascinating stories and takes on things, and it was like going on a tour of her Mediterranean island(s) heritage. One thing she had learned from her parents, who worked harder than anyone she knew, was that you had to push, but you also had to learn to get your rest when you could. To say the ladies had been going on a breakneck pace the last few days was understating all the amazing things that had happened.

Christina decided to suggest that they knock off for the day, and have a quiet evening watching the sun go down over the ocean. She walked out into the back to find Liz and Rica almost asleep in the lounge chairs, and Mable and Marie talking quietly. Marie held up a finger to her lips to indicate they should all be quiet. Christina nodded.

"I'll hustle up something light for dinner and bring it out here. We can eat under the stars. How does that sound?" The smiles on their faces indicated their grateful approval. They would get back to work tomorrow!

CHAPTER 3 – BEWARE OF KIDS
GIVING GIFTS...

Ironically, our children (Marie's and Marica's) unknowingly set up this friendship and this book by giving us a week in California as a Christmas present. Now, even though they work together, we don't think this was a coordinated endeavor. In other words, they just happened to give us, the two sets of sisters, the same days in California and to book us on the same flight. Why do we say that this was accidental (but not coincidental – more about that in a moment)? Because if they knew we were on the same flight they could have been smoother about it – when Marie called and talked to them they were clueless, and when Maria called back, they were even more in the dark. PLUS – would they want us to meet like this – and unite?? DOUBTFUL!

However, we feel that the motivation on each of their parts was to get rid of us for a while. Perhaps they didn't coordinate things, but we're pretty sure they tossed this option back and forth while they were on their "lunch duty," whatever the hell it is they do there. At the very least they wanted us out of their hair, if you will, and at the most they had things they wanted to do without us around. In either case, or if it were something in between, they wanted us out of the picture. That's why we say: BEWARE OF KIDS BEARING GIFTS. There's always a catch, always, and the sooner you realize it the better off you will be!

Now, we said before that our meeting was not coincidental, and what we meant was that there were too many things that "just happened" to bring us all together to have occurred by chance. I mean, what are the odds of bringing two Sicilians and Cephalonians together to become such good friends with so much in common and so much to look forward to? Nope, there was some sort of fate working here. They say God works in strange ways; why not through those two bratty kids?? Something to think about!

Q 1 Why do you think our kids gave us this trip?
Q 2 What gift have your kids given you that appeared to have strings attached?

CHAPTER 4 – OLIVE OIL IS THICKER
THAN BLOOD...

It's really fascinating, and almost eerie, how this book came about. We all met each other on a flight out to LA from Newark, and everything just clicked into place like a slick Hollywood script – except that this all really happened. But you have to wonder if we would have been so compatible had we not all been from Mediterranean Islands: Sicily and Cephalonia. There's something about that part of the world that's unique and distinct. All the rest of the countries half nastily remark that we all have olive oil in our veins. Well, we don't see anything wrong with that. It's what makes us tick – or flow would perhaps be a better word. But it's also about being from an island, where the sea washes your homeland on all sides, and you never lose the feel, the mysticism of the water, and the aura it created over countless decades and centuries of kissing the shore of your homeland. That is what the four of us have, and motherhood solidifies and cements that part of our persona.

Now, we are not saying that Mediterranean mothers are any better than moms from other ethnic groups, but we do take issue, albeit in a minor way, with those groups who think they have a monopoly on pain and hurt because of their children. And, it is often these same groups who think they have cornered the market by doling out guilt to their offspring. Give us just a small break. First of all, you can't spell GUILT without a "G" (GREEKS) and an "I" (ITALIANS), but that is merely setting the stage. When it comes to rolling up your sleeves, 24/7 (justifiably) making your children feel bad for something they may have done, or which you imply they may have done, no one does more bloodletting than us: Italians and Greeks. Of course, that is a metaphor, but not by much.

Let's face it, our mothers did it to us, and we survived. It made us tougher and better able to deal with the world, even, to some degree, to put up with and "guiltify" the bratty children we raised. I know we've said this before, but children, whether they're four or forty, think that the relationship between them and their parents is a one-way street. Think about it, we feed them, change them, get them dressed, take them places, Stay up with them when they're sick, buy them things, worry about the people they hang around with, double worry when they get serious with someone – and all we ask in return is a little respect and concern. Is it too much for them to show us that they give a damn if we are alive or dead? Call the damn house, come over.

We used to get whacked when we didn't do what was right. Maybe we should have done that to our own kids when they were little – or now, when they are big. I know some of you cringe at the thought, but a swat or two never hurt anyone, least of all an Italian or a Greek. That's what kept those civilizations – the Greeks and the Romans – as the preeminent cultures of the ancient world. And that's why we say, today, some two thousand years later, that although you can take the "olive oil" statement as a metaphor, and apply it to any ethnic group, there's still, in our humble opinion, nothing so lethal as a Mediterranean Mother who is out for revenge....nothing!

Q – What caught your attention the most in the above passage? Why?
Q – What can you emphasize using your own ethnicity to get your kids to give a damn about you?

CHAPTER 5 – MARIA & NICK, –
FOUR LADIES TALKING...

We thought we should give you some specifics in our deal-
ings with our children, and rather than going through a long
list of happenings and situations, we decided to use these
examples and show just some of the pain and heartache
they've caused their mothers. This chapter will be essen-
tially a conversation among the four of us, with Marie and
Marica in the lead with regard to Maria and Nick, since es-
sentially they are responsible for getting us tougher here in
California, and thus this book. In fact, in a number of ways
they seem to be joined at the hip – NO PUN INTENDED.
We're sure some of these observations will hit home with
you as we unroll our thoughts, and that you will revisit your
own experiences as you read along.

MARIA –"Well, Maria is a pretty good daughter," Marie
began, "and niece, for the most part," Liz added in. "BUT,"
Marie continued, "for a smart woman who teaches other
people's kids, she really misses quite a bit. She can't under-
stand why I stay in our house, the place where I had my kids
and lived for more years than I can count. She keeps telling
me the house is too big. Too big? It wasn't too big while she
was growing up, did it suddenly grow in size? I feel com-
fortable there, and so what if the neighborhood has
changed? Things never stay the same. She's a hot shot
teacher...wouldn't you think she would know that? Of
course, she was gone for quite a few of those years when she
moved to California to teach and live her life."

"Kind of ironic, huh, Marie? She left for California, and
now here we are IN California," Rica added.

"I gotta say, Marie, she's a good niece, and she tries to
do the right thing," Liz chimed in.

"Yes, she does, she just doesn't do it often enough. How
many times have I wished she would at least call to see if I
was still breathing? And she always thinks her opinion is
the right one. She has no patience with me at all. Let me tell

you, she was not an angel growing up – or now, for that matter. I had to have plenty of patience with her. You'd think she would at least let me know that she cares. And now apparently, she's teamed up with that Greek she works with, and they are working on a book?? God knows what they are saying about us."

"Hey, not to worry, we're gonna have the last laugh on both of them," Mable triumphantly added. "Keep the faith, ladies!"

NICK – "Let me tell you some things which most people don't know or don't care to know because number one they are not mothers, and number two they are not HIS mother. Everyone keeps telling me what a great son I have, and he's done this and done that and he went to such a good school. BULLSHIT. He is where he is, wherever that 'is,' because of me."

"I was the one who read to him, who took him places, who made him aware of things, who taught him Greek, who took him to piano lessons, and who got him interested in the college he went to....and, I was the one who paid for his damn college. ME, I did it. You'd think he would show some appreciation. I had to care for my father, my husband, and my son. Do I get any thank you's, or phone calls, or has he ever taken me anywhere? No, no, and NO."

"Wait, Rica, I don't mean to interrupt, but when you said 'piano lessons' it rang a bell. Did he take lessons on Werner Street, in Hilltown?"

"Yes, how in heaven's name did you know?"

"Maria told me! That's where my house is. Holy smokes."

This is Liz...."As the reader can see, or read, as it were, this chapter is basically four women talking about the heartache involved with kids....we didn't know which way it was going to go, but we tried to get everything down that we were saying just as we said it...another amazing 'coincidence'...time out....

---quick break....get something to drink, your choice---

"OK, we're back. Whew. Go ahead, Marica. You were saying..."

"Thanks, Marie. I was about to tell you more about Nick, but you seem to know more about him than I do," Rica said with a big smile. "I'm just kidding with you, but over the years there have been other people telling me things about my kid that I never would have known."

"You know how many times that has happened to me with Maria?"

"And to me?" Mable threw in

"Ditto...!" Liz concluded, finishing up the round robin. "You were saying, Rica?"

"Well, everyone thinks he's the perfect kid. First of all, there is no such thing. Secondly, they sure as hell didn't consult me on that description. Would a perfect kid go play baseball on Mother's Day? Or buy theater tickets as a present for his mother and then go on a date with his girlfriend so I had to go with someone else? Or write a song and not show it to me first?? It's like he's ashamed to be seen with me. Or how about a phone call once a day to see how I am? How long would that take? Two minutes? Tears and heartache, heartaches and tears, and lack of consideration to the nth degree. That trip he gave us was out of guilt, so he could feel better and, so he wouldn't have to call me. Well, all I have to say is that it doesn't make up for all the things over and over again through all those years of neglect. Heartaches and tears."

Q – What did one of your kids do that was similar to what Maria or Nick inflicted on their mothers?
Q – How do you propose we get even with them?

CHAPTER 6 – GETTING EVEN....
AND THEN SOME...

This may sound harsh, but sometimes, wherever you can actually, you as mothers need to reassert who you are and make your kids take notice, at the very least. They need to be "spanked"(figuratively), so they can see what it's like to hurt and feel pain. This is nothing new, by the way. It goes back to the beginnings of history – actually, to before the beginning of history Just imagine it's ten thousand years ago, and a woman is cooking over an open fire and taking care of her children. Her husband, so to speak, is out supposedly hunting for dinner, although the men probably stopped for a drink or two at a nearby watering hole – a real watering hole, as opposed to the bars and gin mills of today. (Although, we suspect that they had hollow gourds filled with some sort of intoxicating beverages hidden somewhere out in the brush). Meanwhile, the women are taking care of the elders, the cooking, and the overactive children, who find out at an early age that their mothers are the source of food, and cleansing, learning how to speak, and how to acquire the skills needed to grow up. Then, of course, the men come home (sometimes, but not always, with the kill of the day) and it's playtime regardless of the success or failure of the hunt. There are stories to tell the children and demonstrations of daddy's prowess with the spears....but NEVER any help from the damn men....that's where the children get their "we are owed this, Mom" attitude.

Now, we're not advocating physical punishment, which I'm pretty sure was number one on the prehistoric hit parade – no pun intended. Although, truth be told, a forceful swat on the butt now and then certainly gets the point across. But we're talking words here, which, when coupled with emotions and some sobbing, take a grip on the soul which is hard to shake. We are pretty sure that Maria and Nick are not writing about their teaching experience as they claim, but about us, as their mothers and aunts and all the guilt we have doled out over the years. Too bad. If they feel guilty, it's because they deserve to feel guilty. If they had given us our due, we wouldn't be in the wretched places we often find ourselves as mothers, as aunts, as Mediterranean widows, as people, for goodness sakes.

So, while this is not really a "how to" book, here are some tips when dealing with your children. Use whenever the situation is appropriate, or, for good measure, whenever the mood strikes you. The best long-term technique is to start when they are very young. Two reasons for this – First, this will become part of their upbringing, and while they may never consider it "normal," they will figure it's a necessary evil that comes with growing up. Secondly, they will get so tired of hearing it time and time again over the years they will often do whatever you want them to just so they don't have to listen to it another time. (We believe Maria would call it "negative reinforcement") Whatever it is, it works when applied often with feeling.

Here are a couple of examples so you can see how this works. Remember, you have to adapt your tactics to who you are and what your kids are like, but a general rule of thumb, which we are using right now, by the way, is that repetition is always good. If you keep repeating the same thing It may not only get the desired result, but then later you can truthfully say things like, "I've told you this a hundred times" and "Don't you ever listen when I tell you things?" Your emotional tone can vary from situation to situation. Often a loud shriek is effective, and at other times a soft, barely audible tone will have them wondering what you are up to.

You might remind them about all the things you have done for them their whole lives, and are still doing for that matter. "Love" is a keyword. You tell them how much your actions have shown how much you love them, and that all you're asking in return is for them to have some consideration to ease your pain. "Is that too much to ask?" is always a good question to throw in.

160

Q – How would you settle at least one score with your kids right now?

Q – Is there something you wish you could have done differently or reacted to differently?

CHAPTER 7 – AN EMPATHETIC MESSAGE FOR THE KIDS...

We sort of assumed that our readers would be mothers looking for some solace and a shoulder to lean on through all the ups and downs of motherhood. And that's probably true. But maybe, just maybe, our book was sitting on the coffee table or on the counter in the kitchen, and one of the "children" happened to pick it up. So, to be fair, this chapter is going to be written with you in mind. I mean, after all, we do owe you something, cause without you we wouldn't be mothers, and this book would never have been written.

Most children from five to fifty have the preconceived notion that mothers are out to get them at all costs, and that guilt is the primary weapon in this lifelong battle. The truth is, "GUILT" is all we have left to us. It's not that we don't love our children – we do. And we know that for the most part, they love us. The problem is that we need to be shown that love by actions, not words. We realize that you have your own lives, with husbands, and wives, and children, and careers, and concerns. We feel that we could probably help with these things, and instead of welcoming our assistance, we are turned away, and you often use the other aspects of your lives as an excuse for not showing more consideration and sharing more of what you do – good and bad – with us.

How about it....will you at least take what we just said into consideration? The joys you have brought us are the reason for our heartaches and tears. Love leads to heartaches – it's as simple as that.

Q – If you're a "kid," regardless of age, is there something you could do to make things better? If so, what would it be, and do you think you will do it?

Q – If you're a mother, do you think your children, your child, or any of them will follow through on the above question? Hmmm....

CHAPTER 8 – WHAT LINDER DID

Linder killed her mother. Well, she didn't take a gun and shoot her, but she might as well have.. Linder and her mother used to live on the corner, just down the street from us. They were just an ordinary family with a single parent and one child, and they had the normal ups and downs that any family has. Things seemed more or less OK. But then, for no good reason, Linder moved out, and that's when the heartaches and tears went out of control for her mother. Why did she leave? Was it just to be out on her own, or was it to punish her mother? They had a whole big house to themselves, with plenty of room for each one of them to go about her business without bothering the other one. The yard was gorgeous! There was a lush green lawn, rose bushes, and a trellis that Linder's father had built that was covered with grape vines. There were fresh grapes all through the summer and into the fall, and the back porch was a shady place to rest, or read, or just enjoy the day.

I remember running into the mother at the grocery store just a few days after Linder left. She waved to me from across two aisles, like someone who had fallen overboard and needed to be rescued.

"Marie, I'm so glad I ran into you. I don't know what to do."

I asked her what the matter was, and she told me the whole story, how they had a big fight and Linder accused her mother of trying to control her by making all the decisions for her and ruining her life.

"I've had enough. I can't stand it anymore," was what Linder said to her, and the next day she left.

I told her not to worry, that her daughter would keep in touch with her, and once she found out how hard it was to live on your own, that she would be back. The words seemed comforting, but it never happened that way. Linder rarely called, and she never came back, not even for a visit. Her mother lost all her drive to lead her life, and the last thing I heard she was in a nursing home. That's the last I heard of her. That Linder –she killed her mother. And they used to live right down the street from us; right on the corner.

Q – Do you know someone like Linder?
Q – Why do you think children treat their mothers this way?

CHAPTER 9 – AND SO...

We could go on and on and on, as our children might say, but this was not meant to be an all-inclusive look at the challenges of being a mother and the many factors that play into the picture. Rather, we wanted to highlight three major things:

1) How tough it is just being a mother, and how it becomes harder exponentially if you are a widow, and yes, as you get older

2) A mother's love cannot be duplicated by anyone, nor can the heartaches and tears she feels because of her love.

3) GUILT is often the only way mothers have of getting their children's attention, and no one does it better than mothers with olive oil in their blood.

We would like to say thank you once again to:
Gina Micropolis for suggesting this project ...

Christina Micropolis for her invaluable aid putting this all together...

Melissa Topping for turning our feelings into a real book.

One final word: call your mother, or suffer the consequences!!

EPILOGUE

If you'd like to get in touch with us with a comment, a question, an anecdote, or just to talk, PLEASE call us or drop us an email:

1-800-MOTHERS
{MediterraneanMothers@Tears&Love.com}

With love...
THE Mediterranean Mothers:
Marie, Liz, Marica, Mable

CHAPTER TWENTY-SEVEN

It's Never Too Late

(A daily TV show on at 10 AM Pacific Time, 1 PM in the East.
It is broadcast nationwide.
The host is a local newswoman, Melissa Topping.
The program is broadcast live. There are about 300 people or
so in the audience).

> THEME MUSIC PLAYS IN THE BACKGROUND
> With CHORUS SINGING........
> SONG: IT'S NEVER TOO LATE.
> > *Got something you want to do well*
> > *It's never too late*
> > *As long as you start right now*

SONG CONTINUES AS THE CURTAIN OPENS...

SET: What looks like a living room...there is a large
couch and a smaller piece of upholstered furniture, all
covered in clear, thin plastic. There is also an impos-
ing, large marble table One of the features of this program is that the decor is matched, as much as possible,
to the guests of each particular day.

(As the TV and studio audience see the people on the set, the theme song of the show fades out and is replaced by mandolin music playing traditional Italian and Greek songs, and, there are four women, yup, "the" four women, sitting comfortably and sipping dark coffee. The spotlight falls on the host, an attractive woman about fifty or so, sitting on a bench that resembles something you might see at a game. She is sporting a large, genuine smile and bows her head in appreciation for the applause she receives.)

"Hello everyone, I'm Melissa Topping, and I'd like to welcome you to *IT'S NEVER TOO LATE*, where we highlight people who have made a sharp turn in their lives, who have gotten off the bench, and into the game. Tonight we have a special treat: four "Mediterranean Mothers," actually two sets of sisters, who, believe it or not, met their counterparts less than two weeks ago. In that short span of time, they have become best friends, rented a house here in California, charmed the heck out of everyone they met, and written what I'm sure is going to be a best-selling book! Less than two weeks!!"

She held up a book for the camera, which focused in on the cover, which had, of course, the title: *MEDITERRANEAN MOTHERS – THE HEARTACHES AND THE TEARS* a very becoming picture of the ladies, and only their first names as the authors.

"What I'm holding up is what they call a galley edition, sort of a 'scrap copy' or 'rough draft,' if you will, of what the final product will look like. These four women tell some amazing stories in the book, but their own story of how all this came to pass is even more amazing. Let me introduce our guests, from left to right as you're seeing them: Liz, Marica, Mable, and Marie. Ladies, welcome to *IT'S NEVER TOO LATE,* where we highlight people who have made a dramatic turn in their lives, and the four of you have certainly done that. Before we get to the journey that brought you together and led you to our show, let me ask you about the accommodations here in the studio. Does the seating arrangement meet with your approval? How's the coffee? And the koulouria and cannolis?"

"Excellent." "Coffee is great." "Love the couch and the table!" "Coffee and something sweet is the best combination."

"I'm glad you like what my producer rounded up. And he and everyone else seem to like everything as well," the host exulted, as she swung her hand to indicate that the camera should sweep around and take a shot of her backstage crew, who were stuffing their faces with the pastries and savoring the dark coffee. For that matter, so were many in the audience, which was a bit of a surprise to the host. She looked back at her producer, who just shrugged and explained:

"Everything looked so good I couldn't resist letting the folks out there have some, too."

Kiddingly Melissa wondered if he had sent some home to the TV viewers.

"But, seriously, Greg, where are my coffee and pastries?"

Her producer, Greg Harris, was sincerely apologetic as he brought a tray out himself.

"I beg your forgiveness, oh queen of the morning. Sorry, Liss," he said with a quick salute!

"Yeah, yeah, Harris. Talk is cheap," she shot back with a huge smile. It was obvious that the two of them were not only co-workers but also good friends, and that the host was not only quick on her feet but had a genuine fondness for people.

"My producer is really a good guy, but he also likes to draw his salary, so I'd better get on with what I am paid to do so he has a show to produce." Her demeanor was infectious, and soon everyone on and offstage was laughing, which was just as it should be!

"You still here, ladies? Good. Ladies and gentlemen, my guests this morning are Italian sisters – Liz and Marie – raise your hands so they know…and Greek sisters – Marica and Mable. More precisely, they are from islands, Sicily and Cephalonia, respectively. I was introduced to them by the proprietors of a famous local eatery, *Where ITALIANS AND GREEKS Come To Eat,* where I dine at least twice a week. If you've never been there, go! How is the food there, Ladies?"

"Best I've ever had," Mable jumped in.

Marie gave Mable a high five, while Liz and Marica nodded and gave the OK sign with their fingers and their smiles.

"I'll set the stage, and then I'll let the ladies take over. *ITALIANS AND GREEKS* is owned and operated by a married couple, Gina and Ted Micropolis. She is Sicilian, and he was born in, you guessed it, Cephalonia. I believe they are here today…Ted and Gina, could you stand up please?"

Gina and Ted stand up and wave. The studio audience gives them a hearty welcome. Melissa continues with the background on her guests… "Now, this is only one of the many apparent 'coincidences' in this story. Ladies, you're up!"

Liz thought she'd better start, because once her sister and Mable got going, it would be like trying to swim up a waterfall.

"Well, my sister and I were on a vacation that my niece gave us as a Christmas gift, and on the flight from New Jersey we met these two Greek ladies and we started talking, and we became not only friendly, but good friends, and then one thing led to another and here we are."

Marica jumped in. "Yes, coincidentally, my son had given my sister Mable and me the same thing for Christmas, at the same time, on the same flight."

"Coincidence my foot. It turns out that my daughter and Rica's son work together every day, they're teachers at Burns High School – is that right, I always forget the name of their school," Marie went on. She looked over at Marica, who nodded slightly.

"OK, Burns, yeah. Anyway, I think they gave us this trip to

get rid of us for a while, and they planned it so the dates would be the same so they could be free to do whatever...."

A murmur went through the audience.

"'Whatever' covers a lot of ground!" the host observed.

"Exactly!" Marie emphatically stated. "Exactly!

The murmur turned into smiles and giggles.

"What they didn't plan on was that we'd meet. I don't think they would have wanted that. Now we have everything out in the open, and there is strength in numbers, right girls?" Mable interjected.

The four protagonists high-fived each other, the host smiled and chuckled, and the people watching in the studio, including the staff, went into cascades of laughter.

But Maria and Nick weren't laughing. They were watching on their computers while ostensibly on lunch duty. Luckily there were no emergencies, because from the time the show started to the first commercial break, they could have been on Mars. Students were signing in and out for the restrooms, no administrators came in, and the lunch period was winding down while their eyes were glued to their computers. They were so wrapped up in their thoughts that they seemed to have missed Marie's reference to their place of employment! They also missed the bell signaling the end of lunch, and didn't notice the two hundred some odd students walking by them on their way out of the cafeteria.

One of the last kids out was a senior who just had Nick the period before. He stopped at the table where the teachers were seated and asked a very pertinent question:

"Hey, Mr. P, don't you have a class or something coming up?"

Startled out of their daze, the two of them suddenly realized what was happening.

"Oh, yeah, Will, thanks," Nick replied. "We just got involved with a video for our next meeting; lost track of the time."

The student chuckled. "Yeah, they got some good stuff on that show; what is it called – *IT'S NEVER TOO LATE?* Ironic, huh? Since you guys are gonna be late! See ya, Pappas!"

Will was right, as the late bell had just sounded. But, for once in this whole catastrophe, luck was on their side since they each had a prep (what used to be called "free") period coming up.

"Let's watch this down in your room. If we hurry, we can get there before this commercial is over. I don't want to miss anything!" Maria barked with a sense of extreme urgency in her voice. "Let's go, man!"

Nick grabbed both computers and threw them in his bag along with everything else that was on the table, including two packs of Tic-Tacs, a paper towel, and the seeds from an orange he had been eating. It was about 40 yards to Nick's room, and they were there in what had to be record time.

"I think we just qualified for the Olympics," Nick joked, as he threw open his door (which he never kept locked) and dropped his case on his (luckily padded) desk chair.

Despite the perceived urgency of the situation, Maria couldn't helpbut observe, tongue in cheek: "I've never seen you move so fast, Greek!"

"I'll give you a rain check on that comment, Maria," he shot back They both indulged in a quick, much-needed laugh.

"And we're back," the host began with a broad smile. "For those of you just joining us, our guests are four Mediterranean mothers – widows –from New Jersey: two sets of sisters who have seemingly at warp speed turned their lives in a different and exciting direction, apparently helped along by the hand of fate! Does that sort of summarize what's been happening, ladies?"

"You'd make a good TV host," Mable quipped.

There were smiles all around, except from her sister, who chided her just a bit.

"Can't you be serious, just for once?"

Marie jumped in to defend her new best friend.

"Go easy, 'Rica. After all, it *was* your sister's connection that changed our lives, and got us here, right?" She didn't say it in a nasty way, and when Rica looked a bit askance at her, Marie countered with a smile and a quick rebuttal: "As my daughter often says, I was just stating an irrefutable truth."

"An irrefutable truth, and an incorrigible sister, and, I admit, an iconic prank." Marica conceded graciously.

"YES! That would be a great place to start." The quick-witted host shouted. "A great place." She looked directly out to where the restaurant owners were seated. "Hey, Gina and Ted, you want to do the honors? Come up and join us. How about it, folks, do you want to hear a great story from the horse's mouth, as it were?" The loud applause indicated that they did, and Gina and Ted were up in a flash.

"It was like a trip back to my childhood," Ted began...

Maria and Nick were aghast, which is not a strong enough word to describe their state of mind. In fact, only one word would not have been even close to being enough to cover the emotions they were feeling and the questions they had. Bewildered, puzzled, perplexed, worried, embarrassed, guilty, confused, angry, guilty, dumbfounded....well, you get the idea. They had heard from their relatives only a few times, and after that initial night with Maria's mom, all the rest were perfunctory quickies left on voicemails, both Maria's and Nick's. All the calls came when they were teaching, at times their relatives knew they couldn't answer their phones. Oh, and of course, there was the email from the bank to Nick regarding the ten grand, the picture of the four ladies at what were apparently their new digs, and the email to both Nick and Maria telling them to watch the TV show – that there would be some people they knew as guests. Too many moving parts as one of the phys ed teachers was fond of saying. Way too many!

Meanwhile, Ted was relating the "magic plate" story, which had the audience literally slapping their knees as they bubbled over with laughter loud enough to cause a sonic boom.

Melissa was nothing else if not considerate of her friends, and she always went out of her way to credit them with whatever was needed to be said. "Just so the audience knows, Gina and Ted and I have been friends for a long time, and when they told me about the ladies, of course, I was very interested. I am always on the lookout for a great story, especially if it's something we can use on the show. But, to be honest, nothing could have prepared me this fearsome foursome, or the 'sisters,' as they are sometimes called. They are dynamic, personable, well-spoken, imaginative, tough – but at the same time lovable. Their book contains many of their experiences and feelings, and, it looks like everyone here and probably at home has a feel for who they are and what they want from life. So I thought we would open things up for questions from our audience and from those at home. Those of you in the studio who would like to ask something of our guests please raise your hand and one of our staff will get a mike to you. Those of you watching at home, call 1-555-TOO-LATE."

A plethora of hands shot up in the audience, many of them waving vigorously.

"Why don't we start in the second row? Please tell us your name and where you're from, and to which of the ladies your question is directed. Thanks."

"HI. Caroline from Cincinnati. First of all, I want to say thank you, Melissa, for all your shows but especially this one," as Melissa nodded a thank you of her own in appreciation. "My question is to any of the ladies, or maybe even each one could answer? It would just take one word."

Melissa nodded approvingly.

"How would you describe what has happened to you since

you boarded that flight back in New Jersey with just one word?"

"Whoa, that's a great question to kick things off....ladies, what do you say? Marie, you want to lead off?"

"Unbelievable," Marie answered emphatically. "Simply unbelievable."

"Fascinating," Rica added, followed by a different tone in Liz's: answer – "Comfortable..."

"How about you, Mable?" the host asked imploringly.

"FATE. Had to be fate!"

A murmur went through both those on the stage and the audience.

"How about that gentleman toward the back being next up," Melissa indicated. "What's your name, sir, and where are you from?"

"Frank, from Helena, Montana," came the answer from a comely looking gentleman who looked to be about thirty-five. "I just want to say how much these ladies remind me of my mother."

"Which one of us?" Marie asked.

"All of you," came the answer. "It seems as if there's a piece of my mother in each of you. I travel a lot on business and this was the next best thing to going home. Thanks, ladies, thanks very much." His sincerity was evident, as were the happy smiles on just about everyone there.

"I think we'll take one more from the audience, and then right after the commercial break, we'll hit the phones for a few," the host explained. "I don't want to cut anyone short – your comments have been riveting. How about the lady in the third row....yes, the one in the red dress. You're up..."

The person addressed was a very pretty woman who looked to be in her late thirties. She seemed a bit tearful, though she tried to cover her emotional state by stating that she had a cold.

"I'm Sophia from Toledo, Ohio. I was touched by the title of your book: *TEARS AND HEARTACHES,* and I started thinking about all the memories, good and not-so-good ones, with my own mother. She lives in Torrance, not too far from here, and right after the show I'm gonna give her a call. I owe you one, ladies, and you, too, Melissa.

Three thousand miles away Maria and Nick were fixated on their computer, watching every move and hanging on every syllable. Maria reached for her phone.

"What the hell are you doing?" Nick shouted. It was one of the few times he had actually come right out with a statement with both force and clarity. There was no mistaking his meaning or intent.

"What do you think I'm doing?" she shot back. "I'm going to call my mother and get to the bottom of this. This is all unraveling like a bad dream. We send them three thousand miles away and they are still doing it – they are still controlling us with guilt. Personal guilt is bad enough – I can almost handle the one-on-one stuff. But now they're on television, and they've written a book? Who do you think are the bad guys in the book? You and me, bud, you and me."

One thing about Maria, when she gets mad, she gets mad, and it's like a volcano and a tidal wave all in one. She was right, of course, and Nick was vexed and perplexed himself, but he didn't relish getting into an argument on the air, nor did he want to see Maria and her mom go toe-to-toe on national television. He wished he could calm his colleague down just a bit, but, as usual, his intentions were good but his tactics were lacking. He couldn't risk getting into an argument with her in school, or anywhere, for that matter, and she was essentially going to bat for him as well, so he calmed himself down and eased up, which was fortunate for both his mental and physical well-being.

"Sorry, Siggi, I didn't mean to yell. I'm just as worried and hung up as you are, and we're better off with you talking this out with them than with any approach I could take."

Her eyes softened just a bit, and she nodded and put her hand on his shoulder, her usual way of saying that she got it and not to worry. She picked up her phone and hit her mother's key, but of course, her mother didn't have her cell phone with her on the air. The commercial was just finishing up as Melissa welcomed everyone back and reminded the audience at home that they were taking calls at 1-800-TOO LATE. It took Maria three tries to get it right, and then she was put on hold, although when she told them who she was they said they would put her through. She relayed this information to Nick, who was just finishing a silent prayer capped off with some nonstop crossing for good measure.

"Well, ladies, before we get to the phones, I was wondering if I might ask you a couple of things which perhaps some of our viewers had thought about as well."

The four women nodded and said "sure" and "of course" and "anything you want," or words to that effect.

"I was wondering if this adventure, this Mediterranean Odyssey, has changed you in any way, and also, what your plans are for the future."

Mable jumped the gun, as usual.

"Well, I don't know if it's changed me at all, but my sister has loosened up and actually appears to be enjoying herself. How about it Marica? Life can be fun, right?" Mable looked at her sister and laughed, and for her part, Rica just shook her head while trying to hide her smile.

Marie was already smiling and from her countenance looked as if she were dying to get something out, so when Melissa waved her way she seemed to be at full speed already.

"Well I gotta say that I love these two women, and I'm beginning to think that Greeks aren't so bad after all, huh Mable." She gave her new friend a light jab in the ribs, but

Mable was laughing so hard she hardly felt it. "Of course, I'm keeping an eye on that Greek my daughter is hanging around with..."

"That's a good plan, Marie. Greek men are unpredictable, and sneaky, to say the least!." Mable admonished her friend

"How about you, Liz? What's your take on this," Melissa asked quietly. Her thoughtful answer turned the discussion into a more philosophical direction, to say the least.

"I think all of us have learned that you have to embrace life as it comes to you, and that we're not just mothers and widows, but people..."

"With a lot to offer," Marica added.

"And a lot to enjoy," Mable threw in.

"And as for our next move," Marie began, taking the forum back to the original two questions, "who knows. We'll just have to wait and see, right girls? I think we all love what's happening out here. We'll see...."

Her three cohorts were in unanimous agreement, shown by their suddenly quiet countenance and pensive posture. Melissa got things going again with a pertinent yet rhetorical question: "Do you ladies think you're ready for a few phone calls before we wrap things up? I've got Maria on the line."

When she heard the name Marie's head spun around like a top, and the other three ladies suddenly sat straight up.

"Maria, you're on *IT'S NEVER TOO LATE,* but for some reason I don't have where you're calling from. Where are you?"

"Oh, I was so excited I forgot to say. I'm in Pennsylvania. Altoona, Pennsylvania."

A big "whew" came out almost simultaneously from the ladies...

"Pretty town," Melissa added "OK, Maira, what's your question?"

"Well, it's not really a question, I just want to say what a fabulous group this is. They make me laugh, they make me smile, they make me glad to be alive."

Meanwhile, *the* Maria was on hold and her fuming rate was only accelerated by this caller. She smacked Nick on the head with the back of her hand to be sure he was paying attention.

"Are you listening to this fawning, sophomoric drivel this idiot is saying on national TV? Our relatives make her glad to be alive? Where the hell does she live, in Hades? And on top of everything else, her name is Maria. Are you kidding me? Nick, Nick! Did you hear me? Are you listening?"

Truth be told, Nick was half listening, but he was still fixated on the comment Maria's mom made about him, or, as he was better known, "That Greek my daughter is hanging around with."

"Hey, Maria, whatever it is your mom has against me, does she have to tell the world about it? It's bad enough I embarrass myself all the time; she doesn't have to help me. Well, luckily, I don't think anyone has any idea who or where we are. Yeah, at least that's something."

"I would love to have any one of them as my mother," Maria from Altoona went on....

"Is she nuts? Have my mother as her mother? Yeah, OK...maybe I can arrange it...." Maria stopped in mid-sentence as something suddenly dawned on her...."Greek, we're screwed. They do know who we are. SHIT."

Nick was confused. Shocker.

"They? They who?"

"The whole damn country, which includes everybody here. I'm pretty sure that earlier in the show my mother mentioned where we worked."

"Damn, you might be right. Yeah, I think she did. Listen, you'd better hang up. HANG UP."

Maria shook her head.

"The horse is out of the barn now, Nick. We might as well get our money's worth."

Getting their money's worth would have to wait just a bit, since Maria from Pennsylvania went on and on gushing about the ladies while the host was trying to get her off the air without hurting her feelings. As he often did, her producer came to her rescue by walking quickly onto the set and whispering vigorously in Melissa's ear.

"I understand," she said quickly and loudly! "Maria, we are about to receive an important public service announcement, so we have to say goodbye. Thanks so much for your call."

Melissa looked over to Greg, who slid his hand across his throat. She nodded slightly and mouthed a "thank you" to him, and then explained to the audience....

"Well, it turns out the announcement has been postponed for an hour, so let's go to New Jersey, and... another Maria!."

At the sound of the name and the state the ladies just shook their heads with an expectant smirk.

"Hi, Maria. Melissa Topping. What do you have for our guests?"

"I have plenty for one of them I want to talk to my mother!"

Melissa looked over at her producer, who hit his palm against his head three times, the signal that a hard break was coming up – a legitimate break.

"Maria, we have a quick thirty-second break that I am required to take. Can you hang on?"

"You're damn straight I'll hang on...!"

Thirty seconds was just enough time for the host to have a quick consultation with the ladies, and for Maria and Nick to both go at each other and to curse the ironic, sadistic nature of fate.

Melissa had been doing live TV for a long time, and though something like this might have thrown a lesser host, she knew it was part of the dynamics, and often an agitated caller was good for an ensuing discussion and for ratings as well.

"That's my daughter," Marie began. "I guess she's watching the show...."

"Probably with my son," Marica added.

"Yeah, Christina emailed them both, so they knew about it," Liz interjected.

"They're jealous that we're on our own, and doing so well, And we're famous....when were they ever on television?!" Mable added.

"So, you're good to take this call?"

A resounding "YES" from all four of them reverberated across America.

And, across America, the two teachers were so vexed and perplexed that a rarity occurred: Nick calmly made a pretty good suggestion to his co-conspirator, as they sometimes referred to each other.

"Siggi, you'd better take a breath. They have the numbers."

Maria looked at him with the mother of all death stares.

"Nick, don't you realize what they are doing? They are playing the sweet, innocent, heartbroken widows so they can get the sympathy of that damn host and all the idiots watching across the country. AND – they're pointing the finger at you and me so that we come off as the guilty parties in front of apparently everyone in California, Jersey, and everywhere in between. It's the ultimate guilt trip. I'm not going to let them get away with it without a fight."

Nick crossed himself again and again and again...

"And we're back," the host announced. "Maria from Jersey, are you still there?"

"You bet your ass I am," Maria answered.

Of course, thanks to the seven-second delay, which is common with with most live talk shows, the "double S" word was deleted. The "children" heard it in person but it didn't make it to the airwaves. Notwithstanding, this didn't deter Maria in the least; if anything, it got her even more aggravated and revved up as the words were flying out of her mouth almost as fast as the sparks were shooting from her eyes.

"Am I on the air? May I speak with my mother – right now? Or are my First Amendment rights meaningless on your show?"

Her mother, emboldened both by her surroundings and the favorable reception the ladies appeared to be receiving from all concerned (minus their kids), decided to play Maria just a bit.

"Is this Maria?"

"Mother, you know it's Maria. Knock it off."

"Well, we just had a Maria on the phone, and she was from someplace in Pennsylvania. This happened to me once before, about a week or so ago when we were at dinner. Do you remember? Or wasn't that you then, or you now? There are so many Marias, you know what I mean? And it seems that we have two in a row. – that is, if Maria is really your name. How do I know you are who you say you are, Maria?"

There was a tidal wave of laughter once again through the studio, and most probably throughout the country. Except in room B66 in Burns High School, where Nick turned to his colleague with a pale look on his face:

"Your mother's really playing hardball, Maria."

"Yeah, well this next one is going right under her chin," was Maria's quick response...

"Listen, mom, I'm trying to be nice. *We're* trying to be nice, me and Nick, but your 'gang' is off on some wild spree in California and we don't hear from you in days and we don't know what you're doing or anything."

Marie was very proper and calm as she answered her daughter softly yet firmly. "And how does that feel, Maria?

How does that feel?"

Maria looked at Nick, who shrugged. All she had was a "huh" in response.

"How does it feel not to be called, not to be included, to be left out? How many times was I expecting a call, praying for a call, and you were probably 'too busy.' How many times didn't you know whether I was still alive? Did you even care? How many times? And this isn't just for me, I'm speaking for all mothers, especially widows!"

There was an immediate standing ovation, including the crew and the host, who later said she couldn't help but support this courageous woman.

Maria seemed ready to explode, which caused Nick to ask one of his stupidest questions ever, and that is saying a lot...

"Do you want me to take over?"

"Over my dead body," she screamed. Luckily, only part of her statement came over the air.

"What was that, dear? I couldn't quite hear you," her mother stated sarcastically.

"I was talking to Nick," Maria shot back.

"Oh, is your Greek friend there with you? Correct me if I am wrong, but wasn't he with you the last time we spoke? Wasn't he, Maria?"

"Mom, that was during 'college night.'"

"Oh, is that what you call it?" Marie replied with a twinkle in her eye.

Laughter and pandemonium roared through everyone within earshot of the show, led by the host, Melissa Topping, who was trying to control the tears streaming down her face from her uncontrollable convulsions of laughter while at the same time slapping her knees.

She whimsically wished out loud: "Boy, if I only had a video of this it would by itself turn anyone's bad day around, not to mention what a marketing tool it would be for the show!

Oh, wait, what am I saying? We do have a video!!"

Melissa glanced over at Greg, who was holding up two fingers, the infamous two-minute warning till the end of the show. She knew that this mother and daughter slugfest would probably be good for another half-hour at least, but there was nothing she could do about the time constraint. On the other hand, this might be a blessing in disguise, since she could tell the combatants that they had to get in their last remarks, and a hard-hitting summary often made for great TV.

"Ladies, we've got two minutes left in the show. Can you tell each other, and the rest of us, what you feel is the most important thing to remember from your – shall we say – discussion?"

Maria jumped in before her mother could blink.

"I'm worried about you, Ma. What are you and Liz going to do when your vacation is done?" All the while Nick was waving frantically at Maria, who got his message and nodded to him. No words were needed.

"And Nick is worried, too, about his mother and aunt. What are you all going to do?"

Marica jumped into the fray with two words: "WE'LL SEE!"

"Perfect, Rica. Yes, Maria – WE'LL SEE!" her mother shouted out, and then repeated for emphasis. "WE'LL SEE!" Liz and Mable gave a vigorous thumbs up in support of their answer.

Maria and Nick looked at each other in stunned silence.

Maria had a sudden change of both tone and volume, as she softly and sincerely asked her mother: "You mean, you all might decide to stay there, and not come back to Jersey? What about your houses and your cars and everything?"

Liz jumped in: "Details, small details in the grand scheme of things, Maria."

"You gotta take life as it comes," Mable concluded.

Maria was momentarily speechless, as was Nick, which was probably a good thing. Quickly, however, she got a grip on herself, and asked her mother whether she hadn't always been "there" for her. The answer was on point, for an elder widow or for anyone.

"The thing was, Maria, what I wanted was for you to be *here* for me. See the difference?"

"Yes, Ma," Maria answered. She knew when she was beaten, so she figured she might as well throw in the towel. "What do you want me to do?"

"Read our book, and then we can talk."

"But what are *you* going to do next?"

"We'll see, we'll see. Oh, and if you are feeling guilty right now, maybe it's because you have something to feel guilty about! But no matter what it is, or how you feel, you should DEFINITELY go to confession" Marie glanced over at Marica, who was nodding and raising her eyebrows almost to her hairline – "And take that damn Greek with you."

The audience roared with smiles and laughs, as the hostess waved to highlight her guests, who are all smiling, shaking hands, and sharing hugs with their new fans. Melissa is holding the book up and references it once more: "The book is called *MEDITERRANEAN MOTHERS – THE HEARTACHES AND THE TEARS,* and the ladies are Elizabeth, Marie, Mable, and Marica. You can love them, fear them, or be riddled with guilt – but you'd better treat them with respect because you can never beat them!!"

....

EPILOGUE

As of this writing, the whereabouts of the four Mediterranean Mothers is still unknown. If you're ever in the town of Montecito or are dining at *ITALIANS AND GREEKS* in LA, and happen to hear unbounded laughter coming from four classy-looking ladies, please get in touch with Maria or Nick. They would be most grateful!

ABOUT ATMOSPHERE PRESS

Atmosphere Press is an independent, full-service publisher for excellent books in all genres and for all audiences. Learn more about what we do at atmospherepress.com.

We encourage you to check out some of Atmosphere's latest releases, which are available at Amazon.com and via order from your local bookstore:

Finding Us, by Kristin Rehkamp

The Ideological and Political System of Banselism, by Royard Halmonet Vantion (Ancheng Wang)

Unconditional: Loving and Losing an Addict, by Lizzy and Adam

Telling Tales and Sharing Secrets, by Jackie Collins, Diana Kinared, and Sally Showalter

Nursing Homes: A Missionary's Journey Through Heaven's Waiting Room, by Tim Eatman Ph.D.

Timeline of Stars, by Joe Adcock

A Boy Who Loved Me, by Wilson Semitti

The Injustice in Justice, by Charmaine Loverin

Living in the Gray, by Katie Weber

Living with Veracity, Dying with Dignity, by Alison Clay-Duboff

Noah's Rejects, by Rob Kagan

A lot of Questions (with no answers)?, by Jordan Neben

Cowboy from Prague: An Immigrant's Pursuit of the American Dream, by Charles Ota Heller

Sleeping Under the Bridge, by Melissa Baker

The Only Prayer I Ever Have to Say Is Thank You, by M. Kaya Hill

Amygdala Blue, by Paul Lomax

A Caregiver's Love Story, by Nancie Wiseman Attwater

Taming Infection: The American Response to Illness from Smallpox to Covid, by Gregg Coodley and David Sarasohn

The Second Long March, by Patti Isaacs

Me & Mrs. Jones, by Justine Gladden

Echoes from Wuhan, by Gretchen Dykstra

Through Her Eyes, by Maheen Mazhar

ABOUT THE AUTHORS

Maria Orlando, native Jersey gal, well schooled in Italian guilt. Teacher of English for 30+ years.

Nick Pappas - in Jersey his whole life. First generation Greek/American, grandfather, Vietnam Vet, history teacher 30+ years.

*Other Collaborations
by Maria and Nick:*

LUNCH WITH MARIA - A SICILIAN ODYSSEY
(published 8/5/22)

IT'S WHAT WE DO –
SNAPSHOTS FROM 65 YEARS IN HIGH SCHOOL

Made in the USA
Middletown, DE
03 December 2022

16816215R00116